Contents

FOREWORD by Robert Dearden   v

PREFACE   viii

1 Education for the Twenty-first Century   1
Ted Wragg, School of Education, University of Exeter

2 The Confidence-building Curriculum   13
James Hemming

3 Making Schools Comprehensive: Some Alternative Proposals   27
David H. Hargreaves, University of Oxford Department of Educational Studies

4 Political Education and Democratic Citizenship   40
Clive Harber, Faculty of Education, University of Birmingham

5 The Changed Role of the Classroom Teacher   54
John Watts

6 Alternatives in Education from the Third World   63
Lynn Davies, Faculty of Education, University of Birmingham

7 Contributions Past, Present and Future, of Psychology to Education   78
Brian Roberts, Faculty of Education, University of Birmingham

8 State-supported Alternative Schools   91
Laura Diamond, Campaign for State-Supported Alternative Schools

9 The Deschooling Alternative   105
Dick Kitto, Education Otherwise

10 Parents and Children: 100 Years of the Parents' National Educational Union and its World-wide Education Service   118
Hugh Boulter, World-wide Education Service

11   **All Parents as a Resource for Education**   131
     Carol Stevens, Child Guidance Centre, West Bromwich

12   **Flexischooling**   143
     Roland Meighan, Faculty of Education, University of
     Birmingham

13   **Technology, Educational Technology, Independent Learning**
     and Autonomy   154
     Mary Geffen, Institute of Educational Technology, The Open
     University

14   **The Political Context of Educational Alternatives**   166
     Marten Shipman, Department of Education, University of
     Warwick

INDEX   178

Alternative Educational
Futures

Edited by

Clive Harber
Roland Meighan
Brian Roberts

Faculty of Education,
University of Birmingham

HOLT, RINEHART AND WINSTON
London · New York · Sydney · Toronto

Holt, Rinehart and Winston Ltd: 1 St Anne's Road,
Eastbourne, East Sussex BN21 3UN

British Library Cataloguing in Publication Data

Alternative educational futures
  1. Education—Great Britain
  I. Harber, Clive   II. Meighan, Roland
  III. Roberts, Brian
  370'.941   LA632

ISBN 0-03-910518-0

Typeset by Herts Typesetting Services Ltd, Hertford, Herts
Printed in Great Britain by Billing & Sons Ltd, Worcester

Last digit is print number: 9 8 7 6 5 4 3 2 1

Foreword

Robert Dearden

It was through having some small part to play in making possible the symposium recorded in this book that I personally became aware of it and asked if I might attend. What follows in this brief foreword are some reflections arising from the proceedings which the organisers invited me to contribute.

A symposium on educational alternatives necessarily operates with a rather broad criterion of relevance. Not only may we expect a diversity of alternative practices, real or imagined, to be described, but there is diversity also in what such practices are thought of as being alternative to. For example, some contributors broadly accepted the state's institutional provision and concentrated their comments on what might be done within that framework. Thus James Hemming sought the introduction of a confidence-building curriculum and David Hargreaves advocated playing down traditional academic subjects in favour of more personal and social education, while Lynn Davies looked abroad to ways in which productive work might be built into the curriculum. Others, such as John Watts and Clive Harber, implied alternative curricular proposals by their attention to authority relations, particularly in secondary schools. One contributor, Carol Stevens, was concerned not so much with alternative schooling as with alternative ways of preparing disadvantaged children for schooling, while Brian Roberts explored some of the psychological theories which underlie different practices.

Other contributors were less prepared to accept the state's standard institutional provision and were more concerned with alternatives to it. These varied from Hugh Boulter's worldwide education service based on correspondence, through Laura Diamond's campaign for state-supported alternative schools, to the account given by Mary Geffen of the Open University's activities. Roland Meighan represented a halfway house with his idea of flexischooling, or making use of schools for some purposes while providing home education for other areas of learning.

Some of these alternatives have already been tried and, judged by their own criteria at least, have been proved both workable and educationally worth while. Others have yet to be tried, at least in the United Kingdom. Something which few gave much attention to was the nature of the obstacles which lie in the way of these reforms. Do teachers need only to be convinced of their value? Are there perhaps structural, economic or political obstacles which lie in the way, or which reinforce existing practices? Marten Shipman, playing Devil's advocate, fired a Marxist broadside which reminded everyone that rearranging one's thoughts and convictions is rather easier than changing the world. Apart from that, questions of social class scarcely obtruded themselves and even sociologist David Hargreaves did not venture beyond internal structural obstacles and reinforcements in his paper.

Certainly there is a readiness to listen to alternatives as perhaps never before. Dick Kitto reminded us of Illich's influence in raising fundamental questions about schools and about schooling. Indeed, the deschoolers' criticisms generally seem to have seeped into the educational world as, arguably, A.S. Neill's criticisms never did. More material criticisms, following upon the Great Debate, have also added their measure to the general undermining of confidence, for example criticisms of vocational unpreparedness and insufficient accountability to various publics. But I venture to think that teachers will not change their practices, any more than scientists will change their theories, until some workable alternative, developed in sufficient detail, is on offer. Above all, the show must go on.

Why should alternatives to present practices be sought in any case? Life, not least life in institutions concerned with initial and in-service training, would be a good deal simpler if a stable tradition could be arranged. But two broad sources of dissatisfaction provided the answer to this. In the first place there was a concern with certain educational values which contributors felt were not sufficiently recognised, or were inadequately implemented in present practice. For example, the baleful figure of the 'authoritarian' stalked the conference, constantly to be headed off by appeal to autonomy, responsibility, democracy and personal growth. An interesting dilemma emerged in this connection, particularly in relation to Laura Diamond's paper. It is this. Are the various alternative practices to be defended by reference to a different set of values? If so, how do they come to be of superior value? Are they not perhaps just an alternative dogma? On the other hand, if it is not so much an alternative set of values which is at issue but a right to freedom of choice, what is to be said of some exercises of that choice, for example the establishing of an alternative school built on extremely authoritarian principles, perhaps to teach religious obedience and acceptance of a detailed way of life from which autonomy and the like are firmly excluded?

Then again, practices alternative to the present ones might be sought for quite different reasons. It might not be so much that a different set of values is held as that the kind of future for which our present arrangements implicitly prepare is not the future that is likely to come about. Ted Wragg referred to various trends already discernible which might call for kinds of preparation quite different from the present ones. Peering into the future with any confidence in one's vision is a tricky business. It is not just that all sorts of unexpected contingencies arise to upset the best laid plans and expectations, such as the Falklands War and its effects on the fortunes of the Conservative Party, or the discovery of North Sea oil and its effects on our capacity to finance unemployment. There are logical difficulties about predicting what the future world will be like. As Popper argued, the course of human history is strongly influenced by the growth in knowledge, especially scientific knowledge. But you cannot predict future knowledge (since if you tried to do that you would already have made the relevant discoveries, so you would not be predicting). Therefore you cannot predict the course of history. However, even Popper recognised that some kinds of social prediction are possible and indeed his own version of social engineering requires this. How far we can rely on such predictions in constructing curricula, however, is highly debatable, as the search for abilities and skills which are at once both general and of direct vocational relevance makes clear.

No uniform set of answers emerged from this symposium. How could it when the questions implicitly being asked were so diverse? No touchstone, such as 'small is beautiful' or 'salvation lies in home education', was grasped by all. The overall impression was of an activity of educational imagination which tapped various springs of hope. Perhaps we are not, after all, just 'rearranging deck-chairs on the Titanic'.

Preface

In the spring of 1983, about twenty people met at the University of Birmingham's Faculty of Education to conduct a symposium on the theme of Alternative Futures in Education. The idea for such a gathering had come from a casual conversation which involved an exchange of ideas about current initiatives in education that had implications for change and the regeneration of schooling. A list was made of people who, because of their experiences or ideas, were known to the editors as likely to contribute effectively to open-ended exploration of alternatives. The symposium included, among others, parents who had educated their children at home for several years, a former head of Countesthorpe College, local authority staff from a parental involvement project, professors of education, educational psychologists, educational sociologists, and the director of the World-wide Education Service. Because the symposium was planned so quickly it proved impossible to find pupils to contribute from the learners' perspective, which was regrettable. Participants were not invited on the grounds of ideological consistency, and the papers are therefore diverse in the problems they pose and in the solutions they offer.

Papers were written for the symposium by several of the participants and they were available beforehand so that the symposium could concentrate on an exchange of ideas and observations rather than have papers read. The papers in this book are revised and rewritten versions of the symposium papers with one additional contribution from a corresponding member of the symposium.

Ted Wragg does not see deschooling as the answer to our problems. While being in favour of providing options such as home-based education, state-supported alternative schools or other diversifications, he envisages that a well organised, reformed system of schooling is feasible. In this he agrees with David Hargreaves, James Hemming and John Watts. Both slight and radical changes in schools are needed to prevent a disservice to the nation's youth.

James Hemming makes the case for a new approach to the curriculum of secondary schools. Today we need to turn from outmoded conceptions of schooling to the purpose of generating and sustaining the dynamic components of personal learning; specifically, the nourishment of curiosity, courage and self-confidence. The traditional curriculum is ill-suited to this new purpose because it often fails to tap the interests of young people and imposes failure on too many of them.

The aspects of a confidence-building curriculum are considered and are presented under five headings:

1. A thorough treatment of basic skills, including practical skills and social skills.
2. Integrated courses to orient young people to the human situation.
3. Opportunities for creative/expressive activities.
4. Health education directed to the attainment of physical, mental, social and moral healthfulness.
5. Individualised studies through which personal interests and abilities, discovered in the orientation course or elsewhere, may be developed to the ceiling of capacities.

Modes of assessment which are consistent with a confidence-building curriculum are also considered.

It is the view of David Hargreaves that what he notes as the narrow, unbalanced and incoherent curriculum of contemporary comprehensive schools can be dealt with provided we give up simplistic models of school improvement and think out a larger set of strategies; these are bound to be rather radical and upsetting to many teachers. He deals with four possible strategies.

In his discussion of political education and democratic citizenship, Clive Harber notes that there are three dimensions: education about democracy, education for democracy and education in democracy. The second and third dimensions have been neglected in the past and need to be developed by helping learners to acquire the skills of behaviour for democracy and creating democratic climates in schools and classrooms for the practice of those skills.

The necessary change of the role of the teacher from that of instructor to that of the agent of learning is outlined by John Watts. The rapid growth of knowledge and of information technology among other things is forcing this change upon us. If resources and knowledge cannot be confined in classrooms any longer, then teachers will need to be available in other places and will need to be more concerned with the process of learning than with any results in terms of memorised information. The ability to learn has become more valuable to survival and prosperity than most stored information, Watts argues.

The paper by Lynn Davies reverses the usual trends towards exporting educational 'expertise' to the Third World, and argues instead that the UK may have much to learn from radical initiatives in schooling currently taking place in so-called developing societies. It combines three themes — education for self-reliance, education with production and functional literacy — to suggest a model for comprehensive schooling here which aims at schools themselves being productive units. 'Pure' knowledge or even 'relevant' curriculum gives way to an insistence on all pupils applying skills in real situations, and learning, within a variety of pupil–teacher co-operatives, the competence to solve problems and supply needs in everything from music to mathematics, from legal to social services. Through producing goods and services to the community on an economic basis, pupils learn the techniques of co-operative enterprise; they also retain self-esteem and a feeling of efficacy in the face of increasing unemployment and automation. Not only do schools themselves become more self-reliant, but, by making exam success dependent on proven competence at using school knowledge to solve business or social problems, the divide between mental and manual can be broken down. The paper thus recognises the continuing impetus for examinations, but argues that by using skill-based, criterion-referenced and collective assessment, pupils can leave school with motivation in the essential parallel dimensions of entrepreneurial incentive and community responsibility.

Brian Roberts argues that some psychological theories have been especially influential in education, but to its detriment. They have helped to produce and maintain the educational systems that we have, and have created highly misleading versions of child behaviour. He proposes some other models which he argues would be more relevant to education and to the development of children in the future.

Laura Diamond develops the case for state-supported alternative schools. How adults interact with children at school has an effect on how children see themselves, how much confidence they develop and how much they learn. The Campaign for State-supported Alternative Schools believes that the undemocratic and hierarchical structure of most schools and what is seen as their emotionally arid climate undermine children's confidence and stop the schools fulfilling their educational objectives. Though the family is now a good deal more democratic, many parents do not yet see the need for radical changes in schools. CSSAS therefore promotes the provision within the state system of alternative small schools of a democratic, non-hierarchical, non-coercive type to satisfy the demand for such schools and to act as a model for future reform.

Dick Kitto reviews the deschooling alternative which was at the height of attention ten years ago, though the fashion for working within the well established constraints of the school system has reasserted itself, as a case study of one alternative venture demonstrates. Home-based education is one initiative that has grown, and the organisation Education Otherwise has experienced increased support, although the members involved are a very tiny proportion of the population and are likely to remain so. As part of a diversified system, home-based education has a role today in keeping deschooling alternatives in view.

The Parents' National Educational Union was founded by Charlotte Mason nearly 100 years ago. The current director, Hugh Boulter, gives an account of the work in progress. Today the PNEU provides a home–school service for parents who wish to educate their own children. Much of its work is overseas, where it is also involved in helping to establish and run schools. The organisation's philosophy emphasises the individuality of children, the importance of a wide, yet structured, curriculum, the fact that education should be enjoyable and the involvement of parents in their children's education. It is essentially non-dogmatic and therefore welcomes choice and variety within the education system.

The experience of Carol Stevens in working with the parents of 'problem' educational families is reported in her contribution to the book. The project aimed at helping parents to increase their skills in helping the development of their young children. Considerable success appears to have been achieved and families previously overwhelmed with difficulties have been helped to discover new resources within themselves and their situation. They have coped and then improved both in educational and in social terms. The findings of research into home-based education and the experience of the World-wide Education Service, together with the Parental Involvement Project, support the notion that the role of parents as educators has been seriously underestimated.

Flexischooling as a notion emerges from the research of Roland Meighan into parents who opt to educate their children at home. The success of such ventures suggests that parents have been badly underestimated as educators. Flexischooling would allow those parents who wished it and suitable teachers to work actively as educational partners with a contract stating what would be undertaken as home-based activities and what learning would be school-based. Learners agreeing to this approach would develop some of the autonomy found in home-educated pupils without losing out on the facilities available in schools.

Mary Geffen, in looking at the impact of educational technology, proposes that current and impending social changes require radical educational responses. Teaching tends to retain the characteristics that society expects of it; the archetypal classroom experience is still commonplace. Our technological capacities increase; can we use them to help develop autonomous learners who can choose what, how and why they learn? Becoming independent of a classroom and of a teacher might be seen as progress, but educational packages (whether books, tapes, discs or films) can impose their own 'hidden curriculum' on learners. What qualities are required of packages that leave control to the learner? To some extent these capacities have already been defined and developed, as she demonstrates.

Marten Shipman acknowledges that there are at present many calls for change and that some of the ideas explored in the book will see fruition in the future. He recognises, however, that there are considerable political obstacles in the path of reform, both in the general context of competition and a hierarchical division of labour and in the particular context of falling rolls and expenditure cuts. Change will not come only by dreaming: scheming is also necessary and those interested in reform must think seriously about the strategies and tactics required for change as well as about the educational aims and goals.

In between Ted Wragg's introductory chapter and Marten Shipman's concluding one, the book follows a sequence from those authors who focus largely on regenerating schools to those who are more concerned with changing home–school relationships. As editors we would tend to identify the following themes as among the most important that emerge from the book:

(a)   the need for a more diverse educational system;
(b)   a more central role for parents in an educational capacity;
(c)   a reconsideration of the rights and roles of pupils;
(d)   the need to develop non-authoritarian versions of education;
(e)   no blueprint or alternative orthodoxy is proposed;
(f)   a less instrumental view of pupils should be developed so that they are not viewed solely as fodder for the workforce;
(g)   the need to reconsider the nature of work and leisure — whether the future will mean a boom in the service sector rather than in manufacturing;
(h)   social control in future should come through agreement and democracy rather than imposition and paternalism.

Readers, however, will want to draw their own conclusions on the agenda for debate.

CLIVE HARBER
ROLAND MEIGHAN
BRIAN ROBERTS

1

Education for the twenty-first century

Ted Wragg

INTRODUCTION

I suppose I differ from some of the other contributors to this volume because I see the future of education as lying in well organised, maintained establishments of teaching and learning. Not for me the alternatives of home learning or groups of parents banding together to create their own mini-school. Though I am entirely in favour of these options being available in a democratic society for those who have good reason to wish for them, life in our particular corner of the planet seems to be developing in such a complex way that the future of the human race is best secured, I would argue, by a reformed system of schooling that recognises the many changes in which we find ourselves enmeshed. This means more thought about curriculum, better training for teachers and others concerned with the educational service, and a sharp aware-ness of what the future may hold. In the last two decades of the twentieth century our society faces a period of rapid social and technological change on an unprecedented scale. Such is the speed of new developments that society barely has time to adjust to one before another makes its appearance. Since pupils in school today will be aged between 22 and 36 in the year 2000, and some of their children will see the dawn of the twenty-second century, there is a very long lead time in education, and events in school can exert effects for good or ill far into the future.

Guessing about the future can be hazardous, but there are certain features which can be predicted with some confidence on the basis of what we are already witnessing. These include the following.

Knowledge explosion

There is no sign that the production of new knowledge around the world will cease or even slow down. Millions of scientific papers are being produced, and the capacity to comprehend even a tiny fraction of these is beyond any individual. In the Lockheed Dialog system alone tens of millions of research reports are available to anyone able to sit at an access point.

Thus there are three vital assignments for teachers and the implications for schooling are considerable:

1. If we cannot know everything we must know something. Defining the core of knowledge essential for learners at a particular stage is therefore an important skill for teachers to possess.
2. Since we need to be able to find things out for ourselves when overwhelmed by the sheer size and complexity of any field, independent study and the ability to track down and discover information become important. This is bad news for those teachers whose lessons are dominated by pupils' slavishly copying notes from a book or the blackboard, but good news for those who seek to foster a spirit of inquiry and independence in their pupils.
3. When the mastery of anything more than a tiny fraction of existing knowledge in a field becomes impossible, people must work in teams and pool their expertise. A great deal of human endeavour now involves collaboration, and better team work should be fostered in school. Yet studies of groups which we undertook at Nottingham University as part of the Teacher Education Project showed that very little of the collaborative work that one hopes to see was actually taking place (Sands, 1982).

Leisure/unemployment

One million jobs disappeared in British manufacturing industry in the 1970s. During the 1980s the evidence so far seems to be that the rate of disappearance has increased. We need to recognise that increased leisure or non-work time and endemic unemployment will dramatically alter the social and economic patterns of life in many countries. At worst the consequences could be horrific, with millions of unemployed young people turning to mischief; at best humanity could be freed from the drudgery of daily toil, and lifelong education could become a reality rather than a dream.

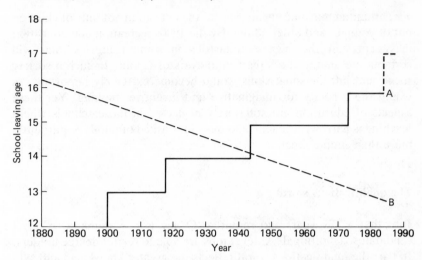

Figure 1.1 Minimum school-leaving age, below 12 until 1899 (Graph A) and age at the onset of physical maturity (Graph B) 1880–1990. Graph B is a rough estimate from data on the onset of some characteristics of physical maturity from several studies (see, for example, Eveleth, P.B. and Tanner, J.M. (1976) *Worldwide Variation in Human Growth*, p. 218. Cambridge: Cambridge University Press.

It is often not appreciated that during the last 100 years or so a quite spectacular crossing of two important graphs has taken place. As Figure 1.1 shows, the graph marking the minimum school-leaving age has gone steadily up, while that showing the age at which children begin to reach physical maturity has gone gradually down. Thus, whereas 100 years ago pupils left school before the age of 12 and were physically children for the first four or five years of their working life, today most stay in education until they are at least 17, especially with the spread of youth training schemes which effectively raised the school-leaving age by another year, yet they may have been physically, if not emotionally, young adults for some time. Ethological studies show that the advent of physical maturity, particularly in males, is marked by a period of aggressive and territorial behaviour. A society leaves its adolescent males underemployed at its peril. The increase of hooliganism at football matches, the heavy participation of the 14 to 18-year-old age group in urban riots, and the recruitment of the young unemployed by extreme political groups all bode ill for the future. Furthermore, any school or college which fails to recognise this significant change, and treats near adults as children, is also creating serious trouble for itself.

If western society can begin to solve the social problems of the present age, attention may once again turn to the education not only of children but of younger and older adults. By the 1990s recreation and education may represent the biggest industries in some countries, and will certainly be among the largest employers of labour. In such a society social and interpersonal skills would become extremely important, as would the capacity for imaginative and inventive thinking. Yet these aspects of education are still sorely neglected in those schools where teaching is narrowly didactic and questions asked of pupils require little more than simple recall.

The qualifications spiral

Jobs that a few years ago required 'O' levels now demand 'A'-level candidates. Traditional 'A'-level jobs are able to recruit degree holders. In part the qualifications spiral reflects the greater knowledge and skill required by adults both at work and in the home in our complex technological and bureaucratic society. It also results from greater competition for fewer jobs, so that employers are able to erect artificial hurdles. Hence the considerable emphasis by some parents on examination success: when resources are scarce and access to the best and most desirable of them restricted to those who have a relatively high-status job, then not only middle-class parents who understand the system, but also those working-class parents seeking an escape from the ghetto, will demand the best possible chance for their children. Thus many parents and pupils themselves, recognising the increasing importance of paper qualifications, inject considerable drive into their pursuit of them. At the same time, less well-informed families either remain unaware of the situation or opt out of the competition. The unskilled school-leaver becomes more 'at risk' in our society than the premature baby, because the latter is carefully nurtured while the former is merely an embarrassment. It is not surprising that in the USA awareness of the vulnerability of the under-educated school-leaver has led to the spread of minimal competency testing to over forty states. It is also noteworthy that the tests in many states include more than the appraisal of the traditional basic skills of numeracy and literacy, having papers on 'life skills'.

Skill or knowledge?

Traditionally, public examinations have put a premium on knowledge. Yet in the society of the future knowledge in itself may have a limited place. If one thinks of knowledge, skills, attitudes and behaviour in an area like health education, then attitudes and behaviour (eating a sensible diet, taking exercise, avoiding drugs) are at least as important as knowledge and skills. If more people have time to enjoy leisure, or work in the leisure industry, interpersonal skills and divergent rather than convergent thinking are of value. Although convergent thinking will continue to be a central part of human activity, it is also highly likely that it will often be *divergent* thinking which solves some critical human problems. Analysis of teachers' questions based on observation of lessons frequently shows that the overwhelming majority of questions asked are narrow data recall.

I once summarised research into the questions asked by teachers (Wragg, 1980). Looking through the various studies of teachers' questions I concluded that, for every five questions asked, three required nothing more than the recall of data, one was to do with class management transactions, and only the remaining one in five tended to be of the thought-provoking kind which fosters the orthogonal leap into the unknown that characterises original thinking. Yet these are the most difficult and often controversial areas in which to appraise achievement or competence, are frequently absent in traditional examinations, and are subsequently less likely to be nurtured in lessons.

Accountability

The political pressure for accountability is now an international phenomenon. Societies that invest millions in education demand some measure of results, usually turning to the public examination system for evidence. Consequently the effects of examination format and content on school curriculum are considerable. One of the likely reasons for the spread of behavioural objectives is the facility with which they can apparently demonstrate that knowledge has been learned or skills acquired.

In the USA, however, there have been examples of teaching becoming philistine and narrow as a result of the publication of unimaginative and safe behavioural objectives. Though some teachers and politicians are reassured by discovering that more children can multiply two two-digit numbers, or convert fractions to decimals, than was the case last year, others recognise that such tight and precise prescriptions can stifle imaginative teaching.

New technology

A whole new series of technological developments could have the most profound effect, certainly by the 1990s. The micro-computer is already well established and is spreading to households faster in Britain than in most other countries. Direct broadcasting by satellite, on the other hand, will offer little that video-cassettes do not already provide. Developments like cable television, Prestel and similar teletext systems may become extremely influential in education. One feature of some newer technology is that it offers an interactive capacity on a scale not previously available. The teacher's authority and control over knowledge are diluted, and by the 1990s pupils will have access both in school and in most cases at home to the largest multi-media libraries in the world. This could be an immense liberation, with whole families able to learn at their own pace at home or in their local community college. In the absence of suitable software, however, there would be a considerable narrowing of education, with emphasis on single and discrete pieces of factual information, little commitment on the part of the learner, a clinical, mechanised form of learning, a condensed and impoverished multiple-choice A, B, C or D society.

Government and quasi-government agencies

During uncertain times in a nation's history large and powerful bodies often spring up to fill the vacuum. In Britain the Manpower Services Commission (MSC) has become one of the few growth industries in recent years, and now has substantial control over the lives of young people. I see two possible scenarios for the future. In the good scenario a benign MSC cushions people of all ages from the ravages of unemployment, nurses them through periods of essential retraining and redirection, and represents an important part of cradle-to-grave social care. The bad scenario, however, is horrific. Most young people receive rudimentary pre-vocational education while a small elite is prepared for high ruling office and command, most adults are on some fabricated, unreal 'job' carrying government-imposed conditions of pay, and most older people receive some kind of government handout. Under a malevolent government of right or left in the 1990s there would be a small ruling elite enjoying huge prosperity, alongside a large peasantry living in state-imposed penury. The outcome would be either complete apathy, with multi-channel televised anodyne entertainment for all, or simmering discontent, social unrest and conditions for revolution normally thought to be absent in Britain.

SCHOOLS AND SCHOOLING IN THE FUTURE

There are many factors currently affecting thinking and practice in education which will increase in importance during the coming two decades. These include the following.

'New' sixth

Since comprehensive reorganisation many schools operate an open 16-plus policy. Whereas in former times a minimum of four 'O' levels might have been required, it is much more likely today that *anyone* wishing to benefit from further study at school will be permitted to enter. Thus some sixth-formers will be candidates with ten 'O' levels studying for university, while others will be students engaged in some kind of work-related course or in the later stages of an MSC-sponsored technical and pre-vocational project for 14 to 18-year-olds. This raises the important question about the spread of ability for which examinations should be planned. In earlier times only 20 to 25 per cent of pupils would take 'O' levels. Current thinking about 16-plus examining tends to focus on some 60 per cent of children, and in practice not far short of 90 per cent of the age group obtain at least one graded 'O' level or CSE, though many teachers would be happier if alternatives to public examinations could be found for the less able. Pupil profiles have their supporters, but of more interest is the pioneering work of Don Stansbury at Totnes School with the Record of Personal Experience, a system which offers pupils the support to accumulate personal files of some magnitude. The research report *Fifteen Thousand Hours* by Professor Michael Rutter et al.(1979) suggested that in schools in the sample with a positive 'new sixth' policy the academic benefits of pupils' staying an extra year were worth while.

Falling rolls

The sharp decline in births from nearly 900 000 in 1964 to nearer 550 000 in 1978 has meant a crisis for primary schools in the early 1980s, for secondary schools later in the decade, and for higher and further education in the late 1980s and early 1990s. Many schools, unless reorganised, will find they have sixth forms of only 50 pupils. Unless favourably staffed they will be unable to offer the usual range of 12 to 18 'A'-level subjects. Already in big cities experiencing more marked loss of population, such as Manchester and Sheffield, the decision to reorganise schools on sixth form or tertiary college lines has been made. As some local authorities have recently caused sixth-form teacher-pupil ratios to deteriorate quite severely, the staffing to cope with an elaborate pattern of subjects could cause grave difficulties, especially in inner-city and rural areas hardest hit by contraction.

Some small primary schools may find they have the same teaching staff for most of the remainder of the century, and the existing staff will have to take responsibility for micro-computers, primary science and technology and other curriculum development. It is hard to see how small rural schools with perhaps only two or three teachers will manage to make progress in the midst of all this development unless they work in federations and offer each other support and stimulus.

The fall in the morale of a force of ageing teachers, most of whom will be over 40 later in the century, will be among the most serious problems with which senior people in schools have to contend later in the decade, and teaching at all levels could suffer.

Localism

The tradition of localism in British education can be seen at its best and worst in almost any part of the country. Almost unique in Europe, the British tradition is to allow schools to formulate individual curricula under local surveillance. Although attempts to shift control more to the centre have increased in recent years, with the publication of national surveys, curriculum framework documents, curriculum reviews and the establishment of the Assessment of Performance Unit, it is still the case that control lies mainly at school level, albeit strongly influenced by examination demands. Some consequences of localism are the proliferation of 'O'-level and 'A'-level syllabuses (over sixty in mathematics 'A' level), the rapid spread of teacher-controlled mode 3 syllabuses, and the existence of 22 'O'-level and CSE boards.

Despite my dismay when my daughter 'did' dinosaurs for the third time in her primary school (I persuaded myself that it was really an example of Bruner's spiral curriculum), I see localism as an advanced rather than a degenerate model. We have reached too early a situation to which many other countries claim to aspire: we trust professional teachers and lay people such as parents and governors to work in harmony to fashion appropriate learning experiences for the next generation. It is a model for the twenty-first century, and if we fail to operate it effectively we should resist the temptation to settle for central direction, but rather find ways of making this mature process, which we have arrived at prematurely, work better.

	Maths	English	Science	Geography	Health education	Media studies	Physical education	?	etc.
Language									
Thinking									
Social skills									
?									
etc.									

Table 1.1 A two-dimensional view of the curriculum. The columns represent subjects given space on the timetable and the rows show other aspirations which arguably are the responsibility of all teachers.

EDUCATION FOR THE FUTURE

There are many factors to consider, and the following represent but a tiny fraction of them:

1. All too often the curriculum is seen in unidimensional terms as a set of subjects in secondary schools or a collection of basics plus topics and activities in primary schools. To meet some of the requirements of the future described above, the curriculum of a school must be perceived as multi-dimensional. Table 1.1 shows a two-dimensional view of curriculum. It is a matrix of almost infinite length and breadth, hence its open-endedness. If we envisage the traditional or newer school subjects as columns, then the rows, which run across all subjects, can represent all the other intentions we might have in education. This concept can relieve pressure on the curriculum, because too often needs to be met are seen as competing for space among the subjects on the timetable given at the top of the columns. In practice some ought to be seen as situated more appropriately in the rows, and, like the notion of language across the curriculum, as part of the responsibility of every teacher (Bullock Report, 1975).

If one thus considers the pressure for inclusion in the curriculum of, say, personal, social and moral education, it can either be given its *x* hours per week like other subjects in the columns, or else one can raise the consciousness of all teachers to make sure children help each other in group work, learn to take their turn during a project, share out the work fairly in drama improvisations, and so on.

The problem of those assignments located in rows rather than in columns is that they usually have no pressure group, national society or school department to support them. Also, people can easily delude themselves that everything conceivable is taken care of in the hidden curriculum of the rows, whereas close inspection might show this to be false. Unless teachers find time occasionally to follow a class around for the day, the pupil's view of the total curriculum is difficult for busy practitioners to obtain.

In the society I have speculated might exist in the next century, the intentions shown in the rows of the matrix, fostering creative and imaginative thinking, getting along with one's fellows, etc., become central rather than peripheral.

2. The development of a properly conceived form of community education throughout the country is essential for the kind of society I have predicted. It is regrettable that, although community education policies are well developed in some parts of the country, little or no thought has been given to the matter in other areas. Not making available expensive educational plant when many people are not at work, when the marginal costs of adult education are relatively low and when the dream of lifelong education might at last become reality, is grossly irresponsible.

3. A properly conceived examination and appraisal system must recognise that lifelong education urgently needs more second chances, more calibration of existing and new examinations, so that there is greater agreement about the standing of a 'pass' or a grade at any level. It is highly likely that in the future a person of 28 will have a set of qualifications such as two CSEs, two 'O' levels, one 'I' level, one 'A' level and one Open University credit. A much more liberal attitude to people with a 'mixed bag' of qualifications is necessary on the part of institutions of higher education.

    Such people will increasingly wish to embark on higher education if leisure increases, and the present inflexibility of many universities and the lack of agreement over credit transfer are serious obstacles.

4. A requirement for all pupils, including would-be higher education entrants, to study across the arts–science divide is important. It seems inexcusable to exempt the highest and lowest achievers of an

age group from the obligation to study science and technology or certain arts subjects at a reasonable level, when understanding of these areas and the ability to communicate well are of prime importance.

5. Much greater stress of group and team work is necessary if a future society is to be people-oriented rather than dominated by technology and bureaucracy. Sadly, the very styles of teaching which endorse this, those so-called progressive methods in good primary schools which put a premium on co-operation as well as independence of mind, have been subjected to considerable criticism by certain newspapers and politicians. It is essential that imaginative forms of teaching which give pupils responsibility, but also involve calculated professional risks, should be supported.

6. In the future the *semi-specialist* may be a central person in many operations of adult life. Since the knowledge explosion we have tended to think of the average and less able receiving a general education in which they learn a little in several fields, and the more able learning a great deal more but in a narrower area. In future the semi-specialist hybrid — a generalist with a good grasp of the wider fields but who has a particular command at sub-expert level of some aspect — will be desperately needed if the pure experts are not to be lost in the conceptual stratosphere and the ordinary citizen excluded by professional mystique. Thus the primary teacher with a deep knowledge of science, or the family doctor fairly expert in exercise physiology, would enjoy professional satisfaction in professions where apathy and stagnation might be a danger, as well as offering a valuable 'bridging' service.

CONCLUSION

Our society faces in the 1980s a decade of uncertainty about the future and therefore about the present. Alvin Toffler pointed out that all education is a vision of the future and that unless one has such a vision one betrays the nation's youth. The solution, in my view, lies in some slight and some much more radical changes in schools, their ethos and curricula, a pooling of professional insight and lay goodwill and support, rather than a dismantling of maintained and organised education. The optimist in me says that we can fashion such change even if the intervening period between hundreds of years of Puritan work ethic and an uncertain future is a painful one.

REFERENCES

Bullock Report (DES) (1975) *A Language for Life*. London: HMSO.

Rutter, M., Maughan, B., Mortimore, B. and Ouston, J. (1979) *Fifteen Thousand Hours*. London: Open Books.

Sands, M.K. (1982) Teaching methods: myth and reality, in Sands, M.K. and Kerry, T. (ed.) *Mixed Ability Teaching*. London: Croom Helm.

Wragg, E.C. (1980) Learning to think, in Nichol, J.D. (ed.) *Developments in History Teaching,* Perspectives 4, School of Education, Exeter University.

2
The confidence-building curriculum

James Hemming

DYNAMIC RELATIONSHIPS

The three Cs of successful education are curiosity, courage and confidence. All normal, healthy children are born curious, as Hodgkin (1976) has pointed out, and they stay curious unless their eager minds are blunted by too much parental criticism or by lifeless or discouraging school experiences. Curiosity is the cutting edge of all learning. It is aroused in children by the stimuli present in the environment and, later, by specific interests.

Courage, for its part, is needed in the educational process to carry the child into actual encounters with the world of people, living things, objects and events. The child who lacks courage, even though curious, may hang back on the touchlines of life, loath to enter the challenging fields of experience where growth takes place.

The third of the trio of basic dynamic relationships which unite the individual and the world is confidence. Confidence is supremely important because, without it, the encounter with life is hesitant and ineffective.

Not only in childhood but throughout life, curiosity, courage and confidence are the essentials for continuing growth. We are all born with the potential to be, and do, all kinds of things, but a great deal of this may never happen if we withdraw from the formative interactions through which, alone, potential can flower. There is no age limit for the emergence of new powers so long as the individual remains fit, open and involved. Today, when we face an ever more challenging future (provided we avoid destroying one another completely) and when more people will have more time to spend as they like, the optimisation of

13

positive potential is vital to personal and social life. Education, then, has the important task of fostering curiosity, courage and confidence in the young as the foundation for life-long growth. If it fails in this, it has failed dismally.

As the child grows older, a fourth C should be encouraged: the potential for criticism, including self-evaluation. But this important advance can be attained only after a sufficient capital of confidence has been built up. Most children are subjected to too much criticism, which undermines their self-esteem and therefore their confidence.

GROWTH POINTS

Confidence grows from the successful use of personal powers. But children vary infinitely in their capacities and interests. It follows that the school must present wide variety in its curriculum, as well as assuring the acquisition of basic skills — the tools for dealing with the world. Only by offering a range of stimuli, in school and out, can we provide appropriate nourishment for personal growth. We cannot tell what stimulus will be a source of growth for any individual child. Hence we should not set out with too many preconceived ideas about what growing points we should seek to implant in the child's mind. Since we now know that everything interrelates with everything else (Bohm, 1980, et al.) any point of entry that stirs interest, and is pursued with fascination, ultimately can bring a child into contact with the whole spectrum of human knowledge.

It is, of course, a part of the teacher's role to open windows upon the world and to tempt the child to make discoveries about himself or herself and the environment, but the essential thing is not, in attempting this, to follow some narrow formula laid down by past habits but to *enfire the child's mind*. He or she will then become truly involved and, through the involvement, grow in relationships with the world.

I would like to illustrate this process of growth with three examples. The first is that of an eight-year-old boy, the son of schoolteacher parents. The boy suddenly and inexplicably became interested in drains. When taken overseas, the first things he wanted to explore were the drains. Where were they? Were they the same as those at home or not? Drains may seem an unlikely starting point for a child's growth of understanding, but when parents are able and willing to answer endless questions on the subject, there is no limit to the discoveries that can be made. What are drains for? Where do they lead? How do they join up?

What happens to what goes into them? Who invented drains? Who looks after them? This boy's interest led him into engineering, chemistry, hygiene, biology, history and geography. Civilisation, after all, is founded on drains. The boy's enthusiasm for drains lasted about a year, but he had learned a good deal by then. Now, three years later, his range of interest is extraordinarily wide, the product of a lively mind and parents who have always encouraged his curiosity and nourished his confidence.

My second anecdote concerns Aldous Huxley, the writer brother of the biologist. Sir Julian, the elder brother, tells how Aldous, still a small boy, was gazing out of the window, across the garden, when their aunt came in. 'What are you thinking about, Aldous?', asked his aunt. Aldous remained stolidly where he was; then, after a pause, answered with one word: 'Skin!'. Skin, as we all know, is a fascinating entity biologically, physiologically, neurologically, psychologically and philosophically. It is, among other things, the interface between ourselves, the environment and other people. Hence skin makes an evocative entry point for a child's inquiring mind.

The aunt, apparently, was nonplussed. One can only hope she did not say something like, 'What a funny thing to be thinking about.'

My third instance is well known. The young Michael Faraday had to discover for himself an interest in science since, in his schooldays, science was regarded as a suspect intruder to the school curriculum and commonly had no place in it. Faraday's private interest might have come to nothing if a certain Mr Dance, touched by the boy's enthusiasm for science, had not given Michael tickets for four lectures by Sir Humphry Davy delivered at the Royal Institution in 1812. The young Faraday was enthralled, sent his notes on the lectures to Sir Humphry and shortly afterwards was engaged as an assistant at the Royal Institution. In that impromptu way was launched one of the greatest of scientific careers.

Let me try to tie things together a little. Confidence is the key to every form of life success. It grows from the effective use of personal powers. These, in their turn, are liberated by reaching and developing the individual interests and curiosities that abound in young minds. Interests and curiosities are tapped by offering children varied and stimulating experiences which give opportunities for potential to develop through interacting with sources of stimulation in the environment. To this we must add that application, the partner of confidence, grows from inner motivation associated with personal interests.

Therein we have the syndrome of educational effectiveness: potential, curiosity, interaction, application, the development of personal powers, and the generation of personal confidence. This is the dynamic cycle of educational growth. To generate and sustain that cycle for every individual child is what education is about.

WHAT HOLDS SCHOOLING BACK?

In order to move towards the confidence-building curriculum we must take a look at the undesirable features of the traditional version. Unfortunately, whereas many primary schools are planned and run to nourish individual development, the secondary system as a whole (though there are notable exceptions) is seriously off course. This is partly because the system is ham-strung by the credit-hunting it exists to serve — what Dore (1976) calls the 'the diploma disease' — but also because theoretically it is decades behind modern knowledge of how human development occurs. Ancient ideas still live on. One is the knowledge-transfer notion of education: the teacher knows, the child does not, and schooling is primarily about transferring the knowledge from teacher to pupil. Another outmoded, but still operative, idea is the *tabula rasa* concept of the mind and education, which goes back to John Locke (1632–1704). The educational concept here is of the mind as a clean slate on which experience, including what the teachers teach, gradually makes an impression.

The contemporary view is, of course, quite different. It sees the child's encounter with the world as dynamically interactive from the start. Thus education should never be only one-way, a passive receptivity. It should always aim to involve the child, moreover the *whole* child — feelings, intellect, interests and purposes. Furthermore, it should always bring 'success in proportion to effort' (Washburne, 1940) so that confidence and courage will be nourished by the experience of learning. If they are not, the incentive to learn will rapidly dry up.

We should also note, in the typical secondary school, the tendency towards intellectual-cognitive excess, to the exclusion of other aspects of human development. Whatever we may eventually find out about the differential functions of the two hemispheres of the cerebral cortex, we already know enough (Blakeslee, 1980) to make it urgent to correct the educational imbalance characteristic of traditional secondary education. The brain is a powerful bimodal organ which should be exercised in all its aspects: feeling along with logic; synthesis with analysis; metaphor with fact; lateral as well as linear thinking; patterns as well as parts; subjective apprehension as well as objective apprehension. This means that creativity in all its forms — the arts, crafts, design, etc. — should not be regarded as frills on a predominantly intellectualised curriculum but should be given the same time, attention and kudos as, for example, maths or physics.

Indeed, if education is to become a complete experience, the old-style encapsulation of subjects will have to go. To quote Hargreaves (1982):

> We must conclude that any adequate curriculum reform must be prepared to challenge the traditional subjects of the academic curriculum, the core of which we have inherited from the last century and from the early part of this. (p. 82)

In place of the old isolated subjects we should offer integrated areas of study which develop many aspects of the individual's awareness simultaneously. 'Subjects' then become components of human understanding, presented in their relationships with one another.

Thus, if our theme is India, for example, we should aim to convey the whole culture and presence of the place: people, architecture, agriculture, industry, plant and animal life, geographical features, history, art, music, religions and philosophy. This is no problem if we make use of modern technology, such as videos, invite visitors in to talk to the students, arrange appropriate visits for the students, and encourage them to get to know Indian families in their neighbourhood. Such lively, active learning becomes valuable formative experience reaching the whole person, and not just a process of absorbing facts. Moreover, facts embedded in a context of experience are much more likely to be absorbed than facts acquired from books and teachers alone. Life-related learning can also lead to discussions and evaluations, which are themselves of great educational power.

Of course we need books in school, plenty of them, but we have to be careful not to be bookish. Indeed, everything we teach should be opened up for investigation and comment. A 17-year-old's view of his secondary school (White and Brockington, 1983) is relevant here:

> Schools should teach you to realize yourself, but they don't. They teach you to be a book. It's easy to become a book, but to become yourself you've got to be given various choices and be helped to look at the choices. You've got to learn that, otherwise you're not prepared for the outside world. (pp. 21–22)

There are a number of other weaknesses of the traditional secondary curriculum which, although they must be mentioned, cannot be dealt with in detail. One is the comparative neglect of personal and social education. Young people are interested in their own development as people and in the problem of relating happily and effectively to other people. For the most part, these life skills are left to take their chance in our secondary schools. The popularity of growth and development courses among adults points up this omission.

The lack of variety in the secondary curriculum is regrettable. It is profoundly demotivating. Young people are hungry for interest, challenge, excitement and adventure, yet all too often the school day is predictable, something to be plodded through until the final bell or buzzer brings the students release and opens the door into *their* world, which is normally ignored by the curriculum.

The standardised pace of the typical curriculum is itself a turn-off. Such a curriculum suits, at best, only a proportion of the students. For the rest it is either too slow or too fast. Too much fragmentation is also demotivating: young people are searching for a coherent understanding of the world, and a piecemeal package of textbook odds and ends is no substitute for this. Fragmentation both enfeebles the appeal of the curriculum and lays the young person open to the lure of false certainties readily on offer in society. The young should experiment of course, but against the background of a valid understanding of society, nature, the world, the universe, evolution, and where we are now. Lacking such a background, they can easily become lost and confused instead of enriched by their explorations.

Gestalt psychology has something to teach us here. It speaks of the figure and the ground: the central object of attention and its context. Each is needed to make proper sense of the other. Traditional secondary education is perpetually bringing an object into the centre for attention while neglecting to fill in the ground. A particularly pernicious form of this error is to put the individual at the centre without paying attention to the social and ecological background which accounts for and sustains individual existence. So we get young people who think that food comes from the supermarket, not from the earth; or who look at the night sky without being touched with wonder at the incredible universe in which we live. The revolt of 'the Greens' and other environmentalists against the aridity of everyday politics is, in part, a protest against the areas of ignorance in an education that fails to give a valid perspective on existence.

Particularly fatal to the growth of confidence is the personal failure which is an inevitable part of any system of education that measures success by the accumulation of credits, whether examination results or some other kind. Credits, by their very nature, tend to cluster around cognitive attainment. This is all very well for those capable of As and Bs, or even Cs. For the rest it is deeply discouraging. As Adler (1932) pointed out long ago, human beings are born into a world where they are small and weak. They strive from the start to overcome the sense of inadequacy and inferiority which their situation generates. In the healthy growth of an encouraged child, striving and achievement will reduce this sense of inferiority to manageable proportions, so that a sense of self-value takes over from feelings of inadequacy. But when, instead, there is discouragement, self-confidence is diminished or destroyed, and either retreat from life or useless ostentation is likely to replace positive striving.

This precisely describes discouraged adolescents. They desperately seek a source of significance in antisocial outlets because their road to socially approved significance and self-value is blocked by the very process that is supposed to be educating them.

Incidentally, those who prefer Freudian or developmental approaches to human behaviour are brought to very similar conclusions. Under Freudian analysis the authoritarian school becomes the father figure and the boy or girl who fails at school becomes the unloved child who learns to hate the repressive father. A developmental interpretation, for its part, would point out that frustrated opportunity leads to anger and destructiveness, or to apathetic withdrawal. The chained dog becomes either abnormally vicious or abnormally cowed. Practically or theoretically, we are forced to accept that breaking youthful confidence is desperately damaging to both the individual and society.

So much for the negative effects of traditional secondary schooling. Let us now consider the alternatives: how to make our schools powerhouses of exploration, adventure, attainment and self-discovery in which the young can find the means to confidence and growth.

THE TRANSFORMED CURRICULUM

A school curriculum appropriate both to established developmental principles and the situation in which young people are growing up, and to the future in which they will spend their adult years, may usefully be considered as having five aspects: basic skills, orientation, creative/expressive activity, health education and independent study.

Basic skills

All young people need help in acquiring the basic skills necessary for effective involvement in life. These are communication skills (including oracy), numeracy, practical skills and social skills — the ability to get on with other people, to share, and to co-operate. These skills require a certain amount of specially directed teaching but should also be developed in use, by participation in the activities of the curriculum and the school community. The teaching of basic skills has to be handled with great care and understanding, as children vary considerably in their capacity to master them. You may find children who are highly able in language and number, and symbolic manipulation generally, but who are stumblingly slow and inept in dealing with technical problems. You may also find children of exceptional ability in all things practical but who find the mastery of reading and writing an arduous process. There are, however, no clearly defined categories of ability.

Educationally, the important issue is not to regard children as inferior because they lack a socially expected skill. Appalling errors can be made in this area, sometimes resulting in children being classed as sub-normal because they find reading and writing excruciatingly difficult, or panic whenever they are faced with a task involving numerical manipulation or exposure to ridicule. The effect on the confidence of children thus rejected is, of course, disastrous. In basic skills, as in all other aspects of learning, children are unique, so standardised expectations are out of place. They need individual approaches in both teaching and evaluation of attainment.

Orientation

Children need to know where they are in time and space, and to establish relationships of understanding and involvement with nature, society, the world and the universe. This aspect of education is essentially exploratory and should be exciting and adventurous: finding out about the locality, including its history and famous citizens, visiting farms, museums and factories, enjoying weeks in the country, embarking on trips overseas, entertaining visitors who have something interesting to share, watching the sky at night, inquiring into the background of the news — what is happening and where it is happening — keeping records, participating in projects, seeking out information, giving talks, organising displays, helping out in community affairs, and the rest.

Such orientation achieves many educational aims at once. It is active, encourages co-operation, calls for planning and decision-making, is a field for the use of basic skills, and helps children to discover where their interests lie. It also develops confidence by enabling all children to make a contribution from their own abilities. To contribute effectively is a prime source of self-esteem.

We should direct this aspect of education not to reading set books or following syllabuses but to building significant relationships of involvement and understanding between the child and the environment of people, things, life, experiences and events which is the setting for his or her existence and participation. Children and adolescents, unless their curiosity and confidence have been crushed, love to be finding out things and doing things. Orientation, or whatever else we may call it, is about nourishing these propensities. The teacher takes part as guide and stimulator, by seeing that the enthusiasms of the children are harnessed to a broadening of understanding and outlook. Textbooks and subject content should be used as resource material, not as strait-jackets.

A special aspect of orientation is orientation to science. Children growing up in a scientific age can easily be interested in science if it is taught in an imaginative, life-related way. This has been amply demonstrated by the Royal Institution at its lectures for young people. Most children and adolescents do not need detailed textbook science; they do need understanding of what scientists do and how they set about doing it. The scientific method is well within the reach of primary-school children, as many teachers have demonstrated. Collecting information is fun; evaluating it can be fun too. Scientific understanding is a universal need and generating it is something quite different from training the next generation of scientists. Those will select themselves by discovering, through the general orientation courses, where their interests lie. Once interest has been tapped, young people become self-motivating and will forge ahead as budding specialists with a minimum of guidance and encouragement.

A middle school (8–13 years) in Surrey runs a mathematics club for pupils with a flair for mathematics, under the surveillance of the maths specialist. These highly self-motivated young people explore mathematics with dedicated application, giving themselves and their teacher an absorbing new interest. They get far ahead of the norm. If we teach in too dull and repetitive a way we can easily miss the potential of enthusiasm in children. The orientation aspect of the curriculum is admirably suited to revealing interests and firing enthusiasm. It provides the ground from which specialist interests grow.

Creative/expressive activity

As Read (1943), Witkin (1974) and Ross (1978), among others, have emphasised, the creative/expressive area of education should have an important place in every child's education and a valued status in every school. Modern knowledge of the physiology of the brain (Wittrock et al., 1977) supports this view. The creative/expressive aspect of education includes art, music, creative writing, drama, design, operating with materials (wood, metal, clay, mechanical parts, etc.) and any other activity in which action and imagination are brought together. In the past this component of the curriculum has often been regarded as an expendable frill and, unfortunately, it sometimes still is. However, today such omission can only be described as dangerously ignorant. The creative/expressive aspect of education not only is essential for the balanced development of young people, but it also serves to bring out qualities that are vital for economic prosperity. The ability to handle materials intelligently and to make use of them in designs which combine good appearance with high efficiency has been in short supply in Britain for many years; this is one of the major avoidable reasons for Britain's economic decline.

The creative/expressive aspect of the curriculum adds further opportunities to those provided by the orientation aspect for young people to share, work together in groups, acquire social skills and make contributions to community life.

Health education

No aspect of education has been expanding more rapidly in recent years than health education. Overall fitness is a complex concept. It includes physical, mental, social and moral health. It embraces home economics, physical education and sex education. The self-confidence of young people and the energy they have available for their own education depend to a considerable extent on the level of health they attain. Exactly how to incorporate health education into the curriculum has still to be worked out, but its importance can no longer be ignored. Clearly, it must have an assured place in the confidence-building curriculum.

Independent study

The fifth aspect is a major element of the educational process: the nourishment of special individual interests to their optimum growth. The interest may be a fascination with bird life, a flair for carving wood, a dedication to astrophysics, or any other of endless possibilities. The aim of this area is to give every child the satisfaction of pursuing a truly personal interest — any personal interest. This interest is not necessarily to be followed in isolation because, in any population of young people, some interests will be shared, so group work can be undertaken. The value of such study lies in the depth of involvement which can come only from a personal commitment, and in the pupils' experience of having the resources that the school can make available directed to the attainment of their own aims. The teacher's role is to act as stimulator, facilitator and guide.

Independent study as a significant part of the curriculum should be possible from about age 13 (Watts, 1980) although individual interests should be watched for and encouraged at any age. In this scenario, the first two years of secondary education (11+ to 13+) would be devoted mainly to a broad, interesting general course embracing basic skills, orientation and creative/expressive activities. At 13 or 14, young people should be asked about where their interests lie and what specialist study they would like to undertake, with reference both to personal interests and to how they see their future lives. Teachers and pupils can then work out relevant courses. This is feasible because, once the school taps personal motivation instead of depending on external motivation — on driving the young — problems of behaviour and of how to keep the young working tend to disappear. Pupils who fail to show any individual interests (experience has shown that the numbers of these reduce as the new system becomes established) can continue with the general course until they discover a special interest.

The principle of independent study has been used effectively at diploma and degree level — at the North East London Polytechnic and at Lancaster University, for example — and also at secondary-school level (Burgess and Adams, 1980). It adds interest to every adolescent's experience of school just at the time when, under the structured curricula system, pupil boredom becomes a serious threat to the school's effectiveness. The openness of independent study also frees the high fliers to pursue their interests without being held back to the standard for their group. We should not forget that many important contributions to human knowledge and achievement have come from young people who were privately educated or self-educated for all or much of the time.

The argument that secondary education has to be rigid in order to secure the numbers of highly skilled people that a modern society needs is invalid. It is just not possible to manufacture dedicated interest: what exists as potential needs specific opportunity to flower. Indeed, compelled learning may be inimical to the full fruition of personal powers. Albert Einstein, for example, had this to say about the effects of cramming on his major interest:

> One had to cram all this stuff into one's mind for the examination, whether one liked it or not. This coercion had such a deterring effect on me that, after I passed the final examination, I found the consideration of any scientific problems distasteful to me for an entire year. *(Hoffman, 1975, p. 31)*

It is intriguing to guess what Einstein might have chosen for his independent study if he had had the opportunity to select a theme!

Another factor which throws doubt on the need for highly structured secondary education is that, when a new area in human activity opens up which requires specialists, as in computer development in the past few decades, experts seem to spring from the ground. All that was necessary was to provide resources and guidance for the young; enthusiastic dedication did the rest. Opening the way for enthusiastic dedication is what secondary education is about.

Because teachers have experienced the difficulty of mobilising bored students, they are liable to get the idea that student choice in the designing of their own programmes would lead to nothing but the selection of soft options. This is not borne out by the way young people actually behave in an open situation (Watts, 1980). Self-motivation is a power for growth that education should use to the full: at present it makes hardly any use of it.

POSITIVE ASSESSMENT

'That's all very well,' people say, 'but what about validation? You must have a publicly validated yardstick of attainment.' Assessment by once-and-for-all subject examinations at 16+ leads to a quite unacceptable level of failure and discouragement, so such a system is really not tolerable either on human or educational grounds. However, young people like to measure their powers and achievements, so there is no cause to reject all assessments as repressive. Rather we have to devise methods of evaluation that are challenging but not degrading. Specific areas of study, such as the basic skills, are best assessed by a ladder of tests, each level of which can be undertaken by a pupil whenever he or she feels ready to attempt it. Success gives a fillip to confidence and paves the way for advance to the next stage; failure is no more than a temporary setback which can quickly be remedied by an analysis of the weaknesses revealed by the test. Thus every child is mounting a ladder of success at his or her own pace until he or she reaches a ceiling of ability without any devastating setbacks. Such positive assessment is something quite different from the ritualised subject examination which may impose an ignominiously low grade on some unfortunate candidate without giving the opportunity for analysing, with his or her teacher, what went wrong. As things are, the examination papers are shredded, leaving the unsuccessful candidates shattered and helpless.

The Kent Mathematics Project (Banks, 1981) and the Schools Council's Graded Objectives and Tests for Modern Languages (1981), to name but two experiments, have amply demonstrated the educational and motivational efficacy of graded skill tests. Such tests are also successfully employed in music, swimming, car driving and other fields of human endeavour. They would, then, seem to offer a thoroughly positive method of assessment for basic skills study. Other aspects — orientation, creative/expressive activity and health education — are most appropriately evaluated by records of achievement. Such records not only tell their own story but also provide evidence about such valued human qualities as application, co-operation and pertinacity. Whereas character profiles are rather invidious and may vary from teacher to teacher, evidence of qualities in action is reliable confirmation of their existence.

There are a variety of ways of validating independent studies. The North East London Polytechnic uses separate external validating bodies at the start and at the conclusion of a course. If students are given careful guidance in the selection and pursuit of studies there need be no failures, even though some students may decide not to complete the course as planned.

CONCLUSION

This paper has been concerned with generating and using the dynamics of learning and with how to free the secondary education system from the examination-dominated, failure-generating milieu in which it now exists. The only case that can be offered against such liberation is that either the individual pupils will suffer or the nation will be starved of the skilled personnel it needs. But no such case can be made. Young people would manifestly gain from a system which set out with a clear determination to develop their personal potential and which built confidence in the process of doing so. The nation would be spared the annual injection of bored, apathetic and often hostile educational failures while being assured that high ability would be positively encouraged and directed within a context not of intense egocentric competitiveness, but of social understanding and involvement.

The last-ditch defence against change — that it would cost too much — is illogical. The cost of trying to control or rehabilitate the mis-educated, anti-social or asocial members of society runs into billions of pounds annually. If the humane reason for change is not considered adequate, then the strength of the case for educational prophylaxis against personal inadequacy and incompetence should clinch the issue.

It remains for parents, teachers, employers and administrators to awaken to the inadequacies of the prevailing system of secondary education and to press for the necessary changes to achieve its transformation.

REFERENCES

Adler, A. (1932) *What Life Should Mean To You.* Hemel Hempstead: George Allen and Unwin.

Banks, B. (1981) The Kent Mathematics Project, *The Institute of Mathematics and its Applications,* February/March.

Blakeslee, T.R. (1980) *The Right Brain.* London: Macmillan.

Bohm, D. (1980) *Wholeness and the Implicate Order.* London: Routledge & Kegan Paul.

Burgess, T. and Adams, E. (1980) *Outcomes of Education.* London: Macmillan.

Dore, R. (1976) *The Diploma Disease.* Hemel Hempstead: George Allen and Unwin.

Hargreaves, D.H. (1982) *The Challenge of the Comprehensive School.* London: Routledge & Kegan Paul.

Hodgkin, R.A. (1976) *Born Curious.* Chichester: Wiley.

Hoffman, B. (1975) *Einstein.* St Albans: Paladin.

Read, H. (1943) *Education Through Art.* London: Faber and Faber.

Ross, M. (1978) *The Creative Arts.* London: Heinemann.

Schools Council (1981) *Graded Objectives and Tests for Modern Languages: An Evaluation.* London: Schools Council.

Washburne, C. (1940) *A Living Philosophy of Education.* New York: John Day.

Watts, J. (1980) *Towards An Open School.* Harlow: Longman.

White, R. and Brockington, W. (1983) *Tales Out Of School.* London: Routledge & Kegan Paul.

Witkin, R.W. (1974) *The Intelligence of Feeling.* London: Heinemann.

Wittrock, M.C. et al. (1977) *The Human Brain.* New Jersey: Prentice-Hall.

3

Making schools comprehensive: some alternative proposals

David H. Hargreaves

INTRODUCTION

You will perhaps be familiar with the argument that the trouble with Christianity as a religion is that it has failed, and also familiar with the clever retort that the only trouble with Christianity is that it has never really been tried. I often feel much the same about the comprehensive school. In pessimistic moments I side with those critics who believe it has failed, but when I see some of the marvellous things which are being achieved within comprehensive schools I visit, I then believe that we have not really tried it. And to say that is not to hurl gratuitous insults at the teachers in comprehensive schools, nor is it to denigrate the ideals towards which comprehensive schools are striving. It is, rather, to acknowledge that we are only part of the way there. That is because most of us vastly underestimated the difficulties of creating a comprehensive school, which was so very much more than simply educating all pupils under one roof; and it is because we did not foresee the array of problems which would arise while the comprehensive school was evolving. We are still working out the meaning of the comprehensive school as we go along, and in consequence we have to acquire the ingenuity to work out strategies to solve the problems that we discover en route.

I do not for a moment decry or seek to dampen discussion about alternatives to, or alternatives within, the comprehensive system. There is much to be learned from such discussions and from alternative

27

practice. But the critics of the comprehensive system have shrill voices and a not insignificant following, and they can be answered only by some extremely urgent and hard-headed thinking and action by which our practice can be brought much closer to the splendid ideal of comprehensive education.

That was the spirit in which I wrote *The Challenge for the Comprehensive School* (Hargreaves, 1982) and it is, I believe, a spirit which is widely shared by secondary-school teachers in Britain. In recent times I have been greatly impressed by the conversations I have had with head teachers and teachers in comprehensive schools, where I detect a new honesty about the problems of comprehensive education and a refreshing willingness to face those problems without defensiveness, without sentimentality, and without any self-blinding rhetoric. The theme of my book was how to create a comprehensive curriculum to fit the comprehensive school, how to generate sufficient curricular breadth to avoid inducing in so many pupils a sense of failure and lack of dignity and, perhaps most important of all, how to enlarge the curriculum from a narrow academicism dominated by public examinations for sixteen-year-olds. I do not withdraw anything I said there and I take pleasure from the fact that many distinguished educationists (such as James Hemming in this volume) have made, and continue to make, similar pleas, in the important task of assisting the evolution of the comprehensive school.

Such evolution follows a complex and strangely unpredictable path, one which is difficult to influence and maddeningly resistant to planning. There are two types of evolution: on the one hand there is the sudden and dramatic leap forward, and on the other the slow, tortuous, bit-by-bit progression. The first kind of evolution certainly occurs: comprehensive reorganisation was itself instituted largely in this way. Curricular change, however, very often seems to be of the second kind. Indeed it was part of the argument of *The Challenge for the Comprehensive School* that curricular evolution lagged considerably behind the structural evolution. But in advocating a sudden and dramatic form of evolution for the curriculum I was perhaps being too optimistic. It may be that I should have paid more attention to the ways in which curricular reform could be pushed forward more gently. I suspect I share with many of the contributors to this book an impatience with the current speed of our development and change, but while impatience generates powerful commitments and a fecund rhetoric, it may be a poor quality from which to develop the cool thinking-out of 'mini-reforms' by which the evolution of the comprehensive school can be nudged along.

THE CURRICULUM OF COMPREHENSIVE SCHOOLING

We can only begin from where we are, even though it is not the place where we would most like to be. More precisely, I should say we can move forward only from the points where there is most dissatisfaction with the present system, for it is here that new ideas will find their most fertile ground. So I begin where there is widespread concern about the curriculum, as diagnosed (correctly in my view) by HMI (1980, p. 6), that we must look for a comprehensive curriculum that shows greater 'breadth, balance and coherence'. But what do these terms, which are so generally bandied about in educational discussions, really mean? *Breadth* and *balance* are often used interchangeably. Certainly they are connected, but it is doubtful whether they are synonymous. The curriculum diet is often discussed in terms of an analogy with a nutritional diet. A food diet should be broad and contain a wide variety of appetising and worthwhile foods, but a broad diet would not necessarily be a balanced diet. For a balanced diet we must take into account not only those foods which are essential to health but also the relative *quantities* of the components, since we need more of some substances than others. It will take considerable skill to ensure that a broad diet is a balanced diet, not least because there may be considerable differences between individuals in the exact contents of a balanced diet.

A *coherent* diet is another matter. Our food intake might be broad and balanced, yet each meal might consist of an ill-chosen collection of ingredients the effect of which would be to discourage eating or to cause indigestion. The educational argument here is that many pupils experience their curriculum diet as being incoherent or *fragmentary*, that is, as a series of unattractive and unconnected parts. The school curriculum is inadequately co-ordinated and too little attention is paid to the curriculum as a whole.

It is easy, then, to agree that the present curriculum is narrow, unbalanced and incoherent, and it is a daunting task to create a curriculum that is broad, balanced and coherent. I must say that in my view the DES attempt to do so, in *The School Curriculum* (1981), is singularly unsuccessful. The fundamental thinking which HMI sought to stimulate has simply not been done. The effect of the DES conclusion to the so-called Great Education Debate has been to reduce the discussion to trivia. For example, to see the central issues as the extent of the common curriculum (or compulsory core) and the extent of the option schemes in the fourth and fifth years is surely to sidetrack us from any real consideration of how breadth, balance and coherence can be achieved. HMI gave a lead to whole curriculum planning in *Curriculum 11–16* (HMI, 1977), the so-called Red Book. They knew the reality of curriculum planning in schools, which is often treated as a matter of distributing time allocations to the different subject departments, all of which strive to consolidate or extend their empires, over time, staffing, resources, and (in consequence of these) status. Such inter-departmental jousting effectively sabotages any serious attempt at whole curriculum planning. HMI thus sought to move away from the conventional subject labels and offered in their place the now famous 'areas of experience', the set of analytical categories by which breadth, balance and coherence in the curriculum might be achieved:

> We see the curriculum to be concerned with introducing pupils during the period of compulsory schooling to certain essential 'areas of experience'. They are listed below in alphabetical order so that no other order of importance may be inferred: in our view, they are equally important.
>
> The aesthetic and creative
> The ethical
> The linguistic
> The mathematical
> The physical
> The scientific
> The social and political
> The spiritual
>
> This list is not, or should not be, surprising; but the curricula of many pupils might well not measure up to it very satisfactorily. It does not in itself constitute an actual curricular programme. It is a checklist, one of many possible ones, for curricular analysis and construction. *(p. 6)*

The list is indeed not surprising, but it is a useful check on curricular *breadth,* for it is asserted that all pupils need each area of experience. If used as a checklist, it might help to encourage greater *coherence,* for HMI resist identifying areas of experience with subjects. There is a blunt implication (though with their typical tact and diplomacy HMI do not express it this way) that no subject has exclusive rights to any one area of experience, and all subjects are concerned with more than one area of experience. Here, then, is a powerful tool through which each department can examine which areas of experience are involved in that subject and thus be led to co-ordinate with other departments which also share the same areas of experience.

That is the theory. The practice, as usual, is very different. Whole curriculum policies are astonishingly difficult to put into practice, as we know from the failure of attempts, following the advice of the Bullock Report, to institute 'language across the curriculum' policies.

The radicalism of HMI recommendations lies not in the areas of experience as such: it lies, surely, in the assertion that they are 'equally important'. If they *are* equally important, one is then led to ask how in detail they relate to the existing structures of subject departments, for everyone knows that subject departments are *not* 'equally important', since some have much greater time allocations, more staff, more scale points, more resources than others. HMI fail to tackle this issue squarely: they do not tell us whether areas of experience should have equal time allocations, and the consequences for departments that might entail; nor do they say enough about the relationship between areas of experience and the hierarchical structure of subject departments. In other words, they say something about breadth and coherence but carefully avoid all the difficult problems about *balance*; and they fail to see that any genuine attempt to introduce in detail the issue of balance would challenge the present departmental structures.

Yet it seems to me that a proper consideration of breadth, coherence and *balance* would have to question the hierarchy of subject departments, for the subject departments are one of the strongest and most rigid structures within the comprehensive school. Communication and change are relatively easy *within* these departmental structures, but communication and change *between* these adamantine and highly insulated structures are exceptionally difficult to achieve.

STRATEGIES FOR CHANGE

How might we reduce the impermeability and rigidity of these departmental structures so that we increase the possibility of whole curriculum planning while not destroying the obvious value of the subject departments as such? I want to suggest five possible strategies.

Strategy 1

We know that all is not well with the transfer of pupils between primary and secondary schools (see especially Galton and Willcocks, 1983). It is widely felt that there needs to be greater curriculum continuity between primary and secondary schools, both to make the transition smoother and to prevent the 'coasting' of many pupils during their first year of comprehensive school. It is also often felt that the transition could be made easier for pupils if we reduced the number of teachers teaching first-year pupils and/or integrated certain subjects (e.g. English, history, geography and religious education becoming 'integrated humanities'). By either innovation many teachers would be forced out of their neat departmental structures, and it is in relation to the first-year curriculum that departmental reins are least tightly held. Through such innovations the foundations of cross-departmental work and whole curriculum planning coud be laid for teachers and pupils alike.

Strategy 2

There has been an astonishing growth in recent years of 'personal and social education' in the comprehensive school. This has not been in response to central initiatives, but rather has been a natural evolution of the comprehensive school's commitment to pastoral care and the need to integrate the curricular and pastoral aspects of the school's work. We now speak of 'the pastoral curriculum', and there is widespread recognition of the need to foster political and industrial education, careers education, study skills and so on.

What is to be included in 'personal and social education'? My list would include the following: religious education, moral education, the social implications of science and technology, careers, industrial education and work experience, political and economic education, community studies, community service, citizenship, consumer education, health education, education for parenthood and family life, sex education, the mass media, social and life skills, and study skills. Many schools teach some of these, but very few teach them all. Even fewer teach them in any coherent and co-ordinated way, and the explanation for this is obvious: the initiative to develop these important features of personal and social education sprang from many different quarters, including a range of different departments. As a result, personal and social education is, in the vast majority of schools, highly fragmented with an unfortunate degree of overlap and duplication and, of course, serious omissions. Given the importance of personal and social education to a comprehensive curriculum, the various elements must now be brought together into some coherent whole. The only practical way in which this can be done, I submit, is to create a *department* (or faculty) of personal and social education. At first sight such a proposal seems perverse, but unless it is given departmental status I do not believe it will be taken very seriously in schools or have a legitimate access to resources. But it would be a department with a difference: one which of its very nature was staffed by people who also belonged to other departments. Thus home economics would contribute to health education and education for family life; biology to sex education; geography to industrial education; and so on. Moreover, each of the contributing departments could then co-ordinate its personal and social education elements with the related material taught in the subject department. It would be a model of cross-departmental planning and co-ordination, and thus would make a profound contribution to whole curriculum planning.

Strategy 3

Nowadays there is much talk of a 14–18 curriculum, but in practice most schools still think in terms of 14–16 followed by 16–18, largely because of the intrusive effects of public examinations at 16. The old division was premised on the majority of pupils leaving at 16, with the surviving sixth on 'A'-level courses. Today, in many schools, the so-called 'new sixth' are in a majority. Many current changes, not least the New Technical and Vocational Education Initiative, are forcing a major shift in our attitudes; we are increasingly being compelled to think in 14–18 terms. Moreover, the recent development of work in social and life skills in the 14–16 years group threatens to create a confusing overlap with the Youth Training Scheme and work in further education, where of course the major innovation in life and social skills took place. Personal and social education must be made coherent *within* the comprehensive school, but it must also be made coherent between the comprehensive school and YTS/FE. Proper negotiation with these sectors should also help whole curriculum planning. This strategy complements strategy 1: our aim must be a coherent curriculum throughout the 5–18 age range.

Strategy 4

It is one thing to create a curriculum that is coherent in the teachers' designs: it is quite another for it to be *experienced* as coherent by pupils. In the last few years I have seen some impressive sets of curriculum aims and objectives, but I have often wondered whether pupils would be able to guess these from their lessons, or even recognise them if they were told about them. If pupils were informed of the aims and objectives which were supposed to be behind a course of study they would, I suspect, often be astonished. The critical test of a coherent curriculum is not the production of an impressive plan but evidence that it is so experienced and so recognised by the learners. I do not see how the curriculum can pass this test unless we move towards a *negotiated* curriculum. By this I do not mean that we should negotiate with pupils the content of the compulsory or common curriculum. I mean, first, that the aims and objectives of a course of study are set before the pupils (itself a rare thing), so that pupils can understand the educational journey they are intended to make; second, that pupils are involved in regular course evaluation to ascertain whether or not these aims and objectives are in fact being realised, and if they are not, why not; third, that the relationship between the course and the rest of the curriculum is made explicit to pupils and subject to a similar joint evaluation as a test of whole curriculum planning; fourth, that teachers make particular efforts to stimulate active learning roles for pupils, with an emphasis on investigational and practical work, on an independent and group basis, so that learning can be connected to their experience. Pupils spend far too much time in school in what are essentially passive learning roles, and in consequence the curriculum does not 'add up' or seem relevant, but remains a confused bundle of disconnected short-term tasks imposed from above. It is surely a sign of progress that pupils of today resist the traditional passive learning roles; it is we who display our immaturity when we bemoan the rejection of them. If we expect pupils to work seriously within a curriculum which is designed to be coherent, then we must re-think the teacher's role and our commonly accepted methods of teaching.

It is significant that the best work on active learning roles for pupils and negotiated teaching and learning has been developed not in the secondary schools but in the colleges of further education (most notably through the pioneering work of the FEU). Many of the clients in FE are disaffected ex-comprehensive-school pupils and it is a major task of FE teachers to undo the harmful influence of the poor education offered to fourth-year and fifth-year pupils in comprehensive schools. I think it ironic that FE is thus compelled to return to the style of the best primary-school practice. The comprehensive school should be the effective bridge between the best primary practice and the best FE practice, but currently it is a barrier, not a bridge. It is painful for many comprehensive-school teachers to accept this just criticism, but those who have the sense to visit primary schools and colleges of FE soon discover, with shock and surprise, that in both institutions teachers have adopted workable alternatives to heavily didactic roles and pupils are capable of sustaining independent and co-operative work of high quality: the contrast with the early and middle levels of the comprehensive school is startling. To put the matter bluntly, comprehensive-school practice has in many cases become an island of bad practice between two sectors which have responded far more successfully to the changing educational needs of our young people. We simply cannot continue in this way.

Strategy 5

No major change taking place in comprehensive schools survives for long, or even gets far beyond the planning stage, unless there is some kind of *structural* change to accompany it. This seems to be an important lesson of past failures. Without a concomitant structural change, innovations are crushed under the collective force of existing structures. If we are to achieve the whole curriculum planning that will yield a curriculum which is broad, balanced and coherent, we must be prepared to consider a range of appropriate structural changes. Here are my main candidates for structural change:

1. The head of the proposed department of personal and social education (strategy 2) must be at least a scale 4 post. If it is not, the department will not be given adequate status to complete the difficult and pioneering work I have assigned to it.
2. In the longer term we must alter the nature of the relationships between departments. At present departments have a hierarchical relationship: those which are seen to be the most important have the highest and greatest number of scale points attached to them. It is these differences in pay and status which are one of the sources of inter-departmental rivalries. If areas of experience are, as HMI suggest, 'equally important', then why should not all the departments also be equally important? If they are, then heads of departments should surely have the same pay. This is, in my view, a vastly overdue reform.
3. If coherence and balance are truly high priorities, then some teachers must be given direct responsibility for them. In the real world of schools unless somebody is given responsibility for something, it rapidly becomes nobody's responsibility. Most schools now give some teachers responsibility for pastoral care. According to the secondary survey (DES, 1979) three times as many schools organise their pastoral care on a year or horizontal basis than by a house or vertical system. The pastoral 'head of year' is a common enough post in comprehensive schools. But who is supposed to look after the *curriculum* of a year group? The answer too often is nobody, because the curriculum is organised vertically through the departmental structures. Surely we also need a head of year (curriculum) to match the head of year (pastoral), and he or she would act as a *course team leader* to create the necessary balance and coherence within a year group. It might justly be said that this threatens to reduce the integration between pastoral and curricular matters. On the other hand, we cannot turn the present heads of year (pastoral)

into heads of year (curriculum), since, at least in my experience, the heads of year (pastoral) are already greatly overburdened people. The head of year (curriculum) would be a demanding post, especially since it would be the task of the head of year (curriculum) for the first-year pupils to forge curriculum continuity between the primary and secondary stages (strategy 1). However, if *both* heads of year moved up with each year group, the co-operation between the two could provide another important model of whole curriculum planning.

4. Under our present system we attach teachers' pay to people, not to the job. In theory people are given extra pay for the responsibility of carrying out a designated task, but in practice one's pay from then on stays the same or moves up: teachers do not move downwards on the pay scale. In other words, the teacher's career is based on a system of *vertical promotion*. This system was developed, and was reasonably satisfactory, when schools were expanding. In a period of contraction it became inappropriate and a powerful source of frustration among teachers. There are middle-management teachers with few prospects of promotion because in the vertical system there are simply too few empty spaces above them.

In addition, the quality of young entrants into the teaching profession is, it is generally acknowledged, rising rapidly, yet it is known that many, perhaps most, of them will not be able to rise beyond scale 2 in the foreseeable future. We surely need to replace the vertical promotion system with a *horizontal rotation* system, that is, a system in which it becomes normal for teachers to make a sideways move to a new job with very different responsibilities. There is no space here to amplify on such a system, but it would surely help whole curriculum planning if a teacher could, within a relatively short period, move from being primarily a member of a subject department to being a head of year (curriculum) and from there to head of year (pastoral). Would this not produce a more rounded and professional teacher than does our present system with two parallel vertical systems of promotion, along departmental or pastoral lines? How can we talk of whole curriculum planning unless as part of their normal career teachers have the opportunity to see that 'whole' from a variety of structural perspectives?

5. For many years practising teachers have complained, often with bitterness, about their own initial training, especially on PGCE courses. This is rightly a matter of great concern. I have been involved in initial teacher training for nearly twenty years. During that time I have seen a great many changes, but most young

teachers leaving their PGCE courses today seem as dissatisfied as their predecessors. No adequate solution has been found and I am not sanguine that we shall find one in the near future. There is an obvious alternative: that all PGCE initial training should be trans-ferred to the schools and become the *entire* responsibility of practising teachers in schools accredited to undertake such work. (This would leave teacher education institutions to get on with the work at which they are much more successful, namely with experi-enced teachers.) The teacher trainers would howl that the schools would do the job badly and increase the conservatism of teachers; the new breed of teacher trainers in schools would rejoice in their new responsibilities and the resources they would be given to exercise them. The teacher trainers would be shown to be foolish for their deep distrust of the profession; the teachers in schools would be shown to be foolish in underestimating the difficulty of the job. There would, however, be one immense benefit relevant to the theme of this paper: the new teacher trainers would quickly discover the need to do something more for young teachers than merely giving them the skills to teach a subject and control a class. In recognising that young teachers need a broad, balanced and coherent initial training, the new teacher trainers would again meet one of the oldest educational principles in the world: that it is when you want to teach something that you discover how little you truly know and how much you need to learn yourself. Perhaps the most effective way to teach teachers to have a better view of the 'whole' is to give them the responsibility for teaching the 'whole' themselves to their young apprentices.

CONCLUSION

I began with what is generally agreed to be one of the central problems of comprehensive schools, neatly expressed by HMI, namely how to make the curriculum of the comprehensive school more broad, balanced and coherent. If the comprehensive school is to have a truly comprehen-sive curriculum, it is a problem which must be solved. HMI bent all their knowledge, experience and skill to this task, and in 1981, nearly four years after the publication of the Red Book, presented us with the results of their inquiry and development programme with five local education authorities, in *Curriculum 11–16: a review of progress*. I find it impossible to read this rather sad account without an acute sense of disappointment, since very little progress seems to have been made. HMI put on a brave front, emphasising some of the positive gains of the exercise and noting the difficulties, but there are few indications of what really went wrong and why so little was achieved.

It is in the light of what I interpret to be the failure of HMI that I, humbled vicariously by this exercise, have put forward a far more ambitious 'package' of reforms. My five strategies begin with a very modest reform: they end with a much more radical and controversial group of five structural changes. I wish I believed that we might achieve a broad, balanced and coherent curriculum for the comprehensive school by less ambitious means, but I do not. To argue otherwise would be to assert that there really are simpler ways of achieving this goal and that HMI merely adopted the wrong strategy or operated the right strategy ineffectively. Instead I assert that we should face the fact that schools (not necessarily individual teachers) are deeply resistant to the kind of curricular change desired. To say so may be platitudinous, yet we continually try to make reforms in the curriculum in a piecemeal way by single strategies that almost invariably fail and then we fall back on the platitude as if we had just discovered it. If we cannot create a broad, balanced and coherent curriculum in the comprehensive schools throughout the land, then we really shall have to look for alternatives to the comprehensive school. But I do not give up, for I believe that we have not tried well enough, and that more successful attempts need not more commitment to change, but a realistic acceptance of the need for a much larger and more coherent set of strategies. I am not convinced that I have found the right five strategies: in this paper I merely place my suggestions on the table for further discussion. My conviction is limited to a belief that until and unless we give up our simplistic models of school improvement and instead think out a much larger set of strategies, some of which will have to be more radical than many would wish, then the curriculum of most comprehensive schools will not become genuinely comprehensive and we shall continue to fail many of our pupils. Without urgent action, the present very slow pace of evolution, based on single strategies rather than a coherent set of strategies, will take decades before we come in sight of a broad, balanced and coherent curriculum. By that time many will have lost patience and will have turned to a more promising alternative species. Time is not on our side.

REFERENCES

DES (1979) *Aspects of Secondary Education in England.* London: HMSO.
DES (1981) *The School Curriculum.* London: HMSO.
Galton, M. and Willcocks, J. (1983) *Moving from the Primary Classroom.* London: Routledge & Kegan Paul.
Hargreaves, D.H. (1982) *The Challenge for the Comprehensive School.* London: Routledge & Kegan Paul.
HMI (1977) *Curriculum 11–16.* London: HMSO.
HMI (1980) *A View of the Curriculum.* London: HMSO.
HMI (1981) *Curriculum 11–16: a review of progress.* London: HMSO.

4

Political education and democratic citizenship

Clive Harber

> Political Education is now seen to have three important dimensions
> — (i) Education *about* Democracy; (ii) Education *for* Democracy
> and (iii) Education *in* Democracy. (ii) means that we need to find
> ways of helping people to acquire the necessary skills for democra-
> tic, political action, and (iii) means that we need to find ways of
> creating democratic climates in our schools and classrooms. (ii) and
> (iii) have moved to the top of the agenda for political education of
> the 1980s. *Lister (1982)*

INTRODUCTION

The central concern of this chapter is political, namely the nature of
democratic citizenship in the future and the role of the school in
preparing democratic citizens. Herbert Kohl (1970) has put the problem
succinctly: 'Power is a problem for all of us. The development of open,
democratic modes of existence is essentially the problem of abandoning
the authoritarian use of power and of providing workable alternatives.'

First a word about assumptions. In arguing that schools are not
presently doing enough to help students to prepare for democratic roles,
the assumption is made that schools can to some extent act as an
independent agent of change. Thus, although schools are very much
shaped and moulded by their surrounding social system, they are not
completely determined by it. The notion expressed in some Marxist
writing on education that there is a direct and precise correspondence
between the social and economic relations of schooling and those of
industrial production, with the latter determining the former, is there-

fore rejected (Bowles and Gintis, 1976). Rather it is assumed that teachers could have a sufficient degree of consciousness and autonomy to play some part in creating future society and its citizens. In other words, schools are not inevitably or only the passive transmitters of dominant social and political values, though this is one of their roles at the moment.

Schools have the potential to contribute to the spread of values and practices more in keeping with an enhanced democratic citizenship in the future. They do not have to sit and wait for democratic changes to occur elsewhere, for example in industry, before they alter their ways. Rather the relationship is two-way: schools can help to create individuals who demand a more democratic workplace and, it will be argued, employers may put pressure on schools to produce more democratic individuals in the future. As Madan Sarup (1982) has written, 'It is not surprising that there are ambivalent feelings about schools as there is a real contradiction in that schools are both oppressive and potentially liberating.'

THE NEED FOR POLITICAL EDUCATION

At the moment schools are not making a sufficient contribution to democratic citizenship. A number of writers have noticed the inconsistency between the stated principles of democracy and the authoritarian nature of what goes on in schools. Harold Entwistle (1971), for example, sees a contradiction between what the school teaches and what is expected of an individual in a democracy. He argues that political socialisation research shows that the school encourages a quietist/passive conception of political participation, emphasising the individual's role as subject rather than active citizen. He concludes that 'We seem to be saying to the young, "prepare yourself for active, adult citizenship but be deferential and obedient as children".'

Until recently schools seem to have been doing even less than the minimum required of them in a democracy. At the very least, students who will be able to vote at eighteen should have enough knowledge about the political system to be able to make a real choice in elections and to be sensitive to the biases and distortions of the media. Yet a survey of the political knowledge of school-leavers in the mid-1970s revealed widespread political ignorance, and it is no comfort to know that the evidence suggests that this persists into adult life (Stradling,

1977). Clearly, schooling has done little to alleviate political ignorance and confusion among the electorate.

Some, however, would argue that political ignorance does not matter and that for democracy to function there must be a sufficient proportion of the citizenry who are politically ignorant and politically passive. Otherwise, so the argument goes, too many demands would be made on the political system, causing it to overload and become unstable. Yet it can be countered that there are good reasons why political ignorance is bad for a democratic system. Jay Blumler (1974) has suggested three such reasons:

1. An ill-informed electorate tends to put pressure on governments to adopt ill-conceived and undesirable politics.
2. Many government policies can only be effective if the public comprehends and accepts them.
3. A politically ignorant population is easily manipulated.

To these Robert Stradling (1977) has added a fourth: that a populace which does not understand the problems facing a government may not only make undesirable demands on the government, it may also make contradictory and even impossible demands and push these to the point of political breakdown.

This second set of arguments seem to have been more telling, as there has been growing discussion in official circles since the mid-1970s on the need for political education of the young (Brennan, 1981). The desire for this may stem from a fear that young people are deserting the traditional political parties and being attracted to 'extremist' groups such as the National Front and the Socialist Workers Party, but it does seem to have had an effect on schools. Since 1977, when HMI published a working paper on political education, the number of schools offering courses on politics has doubled (*Times Educational Supplement*, 1982).

School courses in politics may be useful in providing the minimum level of political *knowledge* necessary to be able to make some sort of meaningful electoral choice, but a more important question is whether they can provide the political *skills* necessary for a greater ability to participate. Such skills are essential if future citizens are to be more able to defend themselves politically and to avoid manipulation. For example, will students as future citizens have the ability and confidence to resist if a council closes down a popular local amenity? How would they go about influencing those who make the decisions? Without political skills the citizen is reduced to a spectator, unable effectively to support a cause or defend an interest even when the issue is of immediate concern.

Yet many feel that school is doing little to provide such skills. One group suggests that 'It would be naive to suggest that schools of the present inflexible type could produce enlightened responsible citizens, able to exercise their democratic rights' (White, 1976/77). John Watts (1980) regards this as a serious problem, as he sees subservience to authoritarianism, the abdication of personal responsibility and the loss of freedom as major threats to the individual in the society of AD 2000. In order to defend themselves against this, citizens must have a confidence in self-identity, a readiness to face the unknown without fear, a capacity for identifying and solving new problems and an ability to collaborate by handling the interaction of the self and others. He concludes that no list of basic skills can overlook these essentials for survival.

One set of democratic political skills has been suggested by Robert Stradling in Porter (1979). These are as follows:

1. Interpret and evaluate political information and evidence.
2. Organise information through basic political concepts and generalisations.
3. Apply reasoning skills to political problems and construct sound arguments based on evidence.
4. Perceive consequences of taking or not taking specific political action in given contexts.
5. Express one's own interests, beliefs and viewpoints through an appropriate medium.
6. Participate in political discussion and debate.
7. Perceive and understand (if not agree with) the interests, beliefs and views of others.
8. Exercise empathy (to imagine what it might be like to be in someone else's shoes).
9. Participate in group decision-making.
10. Effectively influence and/or change political situations.

If schools of the future are to contribute to the creation of a citizenry better able to influence those with power and hence to make them more accountable, then they must consciously make an effort to develop such skills (Smith, 1981). Some implications for classroom practice, wider school organisation and the school's contact with the community are discussed below. It should be noted here, however, that it is not only a case of the schools attempting to bring about change by creating a citizenry better able to participate and hence to shape its own affairs between elections. It could equally well be argued that in the relatively near future society is going to need citizens who possess such political skills. In 1979 Pat White argued that political education was necessary in order to meet growing trends towards workplace democracy such as those manifested in the growth of co-operatives and the Bullock Report. In 1982, although there were differences of emphasis, the major political parties seemed to be unanimous in their support for the idea of industrial democracy which would establish new arrangements for consultation, participation and involvement of employees in the orga- nisations for which they work. For example, Mr Tebbit, the Secretary of State for Employment, argued in October 1981 that society today is less deferential than it used to be and that employees resent the old authoritarian paternalism and the 'them and us' approach. He suggested that if employees are treated as responsible individuals who have as much of an interest in the firm's prosperity as the proprietors, they may well respond in terms of both productivity and ideas on how to improve the firm (Thomas, 1982).

If this is to be a trend of the future, what are the schools doing to aid pupils in developing democratic political skills? At the moment the answer is probably 'very little'. The general nature of classroom and school-wide relationships at present is best described as 'bureaucratic– authoritarian'. Marten Shipman (1971) describes this well when he suggests that:

> Personal happiness and emotional stability remain dependent on satisfactory family life. Competence and personal achievement have become increasingly the product of adequate schooling. Punctu- ality, quiet, orderly work in large groups, response to orders, bells and timetables, respect for authority, even tolerance of monotony, boredom, punishment, lack of reward and regular attendance at place of work are habits to be learned in school.

Classroom method is most often about the transmission of knowledge from the teacher as expert, with 'factual' answers that are either right or wrong. Open discussion of values and ideas is rare and what is characterised as discussion is more likely to be teacher-led question and answer. The school, on the other hand, is about rules which the student takes no part in forming and which therefore do much to enhance dependence and little to encourage individual responsibility. It is also worth noting that this situation differs considerably from the public schools' emphasis on skills to increase responsibility and build confi- dence. To date the public schools have been very successful at politically educating a social class that has the confidence, knowledge, skills and expectations to defend its own interests (Brennan, 1981).

There are many changes that are necessary if the school is to play a part in equipping a future citizenry with democratic political skills. One such change, for example, is in the form and use of assessment. This is a problem often ignored by those seeking change but is in fact a major obstacle, as so much of schooling revolves around it. Elsewhere I have argued for more varied and flexible approaches to the assessment of political skills (Harber, 1983). The discussion that follows, however, concentrates on changes required in classroom climate and school organisation.

These changes all point in the direction of more open and less authoritarian relationships in schools. The irony is that the most immediate pressure for such change may come from a problem that horrifies most people in education, that of the rising tide of youth unemployment. Authoritarian structures geared to examination success may work when the job market is buoyant, but their legitimacy is seriously undermined when there are few or no jobs to be had. As one Birmingham head put it, 'Thinking fourth and fifth formers are beginning to ask what is it all for? If they like the school, or a particular subject, then they will not rebel. But I wonder how long we will get away with it' (*Guardian*, 1982).

CLASSROOM CLIMATE

One of the most conclusive findings of political socialisation research has been that an open or democratic classroom environment fosters a range of positive political attitudes such as greater political interest, less authoritarianism, greater political knowledge and greater political efficacy (Ehman, 1977). This begs the important question asked by the Political Education Research Unit at York University: 'What would a democratic classroom look like?' (Allen). There is something of a problem here. Clearly democracy implies choice, yet completely free choice can mean that learning is totally individualised. However, if such political skills as the construction of arguments, the expression of interests, group decision-making, etc. are to be achieved, then students must be free to exchange values, ideas, views and opinions about political issues in the classroom. In short, discussion is very important. The democratic classroom requires a compromise between the individual and the group. Some agreed areas must be explored in common. Some political skills may be developed on an individual basis but most, especially those more closely related to action, need to be developed in a group setting. Interestingly, it has been argued that the problem structuring and group problem-solving skills learned in this way are at the heart of what is required in harnessing the technology of a future characterised by change and uncertainty (Virgo, 1982). The following, therefore, will concentrate on discussion and group work in the classroom.

In trying to answer the question 'What is discussion?', David Bridges (1979) has argued that discussion involves the putting forward of more than one point of view in order to improve knowledge and understanding. There does not have to be any final judgement, as the purpose may be simply to illuminate alternatives. However, an essential ingredient is the mutual responsiveness of the participants in the discussion, i.e. that what is said earlier affects what is said later and that it is not just a case of individuals making statements. Hence discussion needs a disposition to understand, appreciate and be affected by the range of opinions offered. It is not a single-minded defence of one's own position but rather a give-and-take activity.

The classroom climate conducive to discussion is as much about 'how' people think as 'what' they think. The Programme for Political Education identified a series of what it termed 'procedural values' such as freedom, toleration, fairness and respect for evidence and reasoning that it considered necessary as ground rules for classroom political education (Porter, 1979). The aim is to move from the 'closed' to the 'open' mind, as outlined in the following checklist (World Studies Project, 1979).

Tendencies of the 'closed' mind	*Tendencies of the 'open' mind*
Inconsistency between what a person says and what they do	To acknowledge that one is inconsistent, and to try to bring theory and practice together
'Black and white' thinking — 'we're all right, they're all wrong'	Acceptance that 'there's right and wrong on both sides'
Not much knowledge about issues on which one nevertheless has strong views	A lot of knowledge of relevant facts, including facts which don't support one's own view
Not prepared to change one's mind — e.g. 'don't confuse me with the facts'	Prepared to change one's mind in the light of new evidence
To make generalisations on the basis of anecdotal examples	To use anecdotes as illustrations, but not as evidence
To appeal to authority — 'everybody agrees . . . ', 'so and so says so . . . ', 'it's in the newspaper . . . '	To appeal to evidence
To attack integrity or sanity of people with other views — 'anyone who thinks that needs their head seeing to'	To retain respect for, and to avoid insulting, people with whom one disagrees
Not to mix socially with people of other views, and to avoid reading newspapers etc. with which one doesn't agree	To welcome opportunities for argument with others in order to clarify one's own thinking

| Not to be able to imagine the feelings of people with whom one disagrees | Being able to empathise with people with whom one disagrees |

The 'open' mind is very much a target to be aimed at and readers will no doubt recognise that they fail to live up to the standards set. Yet the following examples, observed in classrooms by the Political Education Research Unit, give an indication of what is to be avoided. This is especially so in respect of 'teacher closure', that is where teachers deny opportunity for dialogue and discussion for no obviously good reason (Allen). In one class an observed student asked, 'How can one MP represent all his constituents?' (i.e. when the constituents disagree with each other). The teacher replied, 'You have lost your thread, you under-aged cretin'. In another case a student asked, 'What if there is a disagreement among teachers about how the school's money is spent?' and got the answer, 'No problem — we are all very reasonable people'. When a student raised the possibility that the police contained both good and bad individuals, the teacher replied, 'The police rely on our co-operation. They are doing something which benefits all of us' and then moved away from the discussion. One student described what socialism was for him and the teacher responded 'Oh — that's a load of crap . . . with the greatest of respect'.

A common reaction to the suggestion that young people should be involved in discussing controversial political issues in the classroom is the accusation of bias, that there is a risk that they will be indoctrinated by their teachers. This is an insufficient reason for excluding political education on a number of counts. First, young people are constantly exposed to biased political material in the family, in the newspapers, on television and in their reading. Political socialisation research shows clearly that school students begin to develop political values and attitudes from as young as four or five years old and that this precedes any knowledge on which to base them (Stacey, 1978). Indeed, it has been shown clearly that pupils leave school at 16 with definite political attitudes and very limited political knowledge: a majority of a sample of 15-year-olds thought that the IRA was a Protestant organisation set up to prevent Ulster being united with Ireland (Stradling, 1977). Political education could do much to promote a more balanced, coherent and systematic approach to politics than the haphazard, one-sided political socialisation that takes place in the family and the media. It could also help students to perceive bias and values in their sources of political learning. A second point is that the school is itself a source of political learning. In the case of the 'hidden curriculum' students learn political lessons from the authority structure of the school, the nature of interaction in the classroom, the organisation of the timetable, etc. The overt timetable, on the other hand, contains many areas directly concerned with controversial values. The more obvious are perhaps English, RE, geography and history, though other subjects like music and science are not without values and controversies (Whitty and Young, 1976). It could be argued that the real danger of bias comes not from those subjects which deal with controversial material but where the teacher may be less aware of the problem than teachers involved in explicit political education.

Nevertheless, even if the risk of bias is an insufficient reason for excluding political education, there are very real organisational problems in handling classroom discussion successfully. It is perhaps not surprising that some of the best practical advice on this, including the crucial consideration of the reduction in the role of the teacher as 'expert', comes from a teaching project based in Northern Ireland (Schools Cultural Studies Project). An interesting point noted by the Political Education Research Unit was that many teachers they observed used role-play games to provoke discussion and to encourage empathy. However, PERU felt that often these did not go beyond attempts to deduce *intellectually* what another person's position might be, that is, there was no sign of *emotional* identification (Allen). One way round this is the series of 'experiential' learning games developed by David Selby (1984), where students feel what it is like to be in certain roles.

THE SCHOOL

Many would argue that the open type of classroom necessary for a discursive, explorative form of political education cannot be achieved in the context of an authoritarian school structure. Kohl (1970) has given some useful advice on how it can be done using teacher autonomy in the classroom, but a number of his assumptions (teacher influence over the timetable, one teacher based in one classroom, open stretches of time, etc.) do not seem readily applicable to British secondary schools. While not suggesting that the teacher cannot use classroom autonomy to his or her advantage, there is little doubt that political education would be helped by a more open and democratic school structure.

The case for a more democratic form of schooling was put clearly by the Schools Council in *The Practical Curriculum* (1981):

> Some values, like those of democracy, tolerance and responsibility, grow only with experience of them. Social education arises from a school's ethos, its organisation and its relations with the community . . . Schools need to practise what they seek to promote.

Student involvement in school decision-making is necessary because people have to learn the political skills to operate democratic institutions; they do not come naturally.

A number of benefits should stem from a more democratic form of school organisation, mainly in terms of the school being run more efficiently, smoothly and fairly. First, rules are likely to be kept better if they are democratically agreed to in the first place. Second, the aim is to increase the sense of self-discipline and responsibility, as students will have more control over their own organisation. Third, decision-making is improved as a wider range of interests and opinions is considered. Fourth, intra-school communications are improved.

Many of the arguments against using school organisation for enhancing democratic learning accept that as an aim it might be desirable, but argue that the practical problems are too great for its successful operation. Harold Entwistle (1971) brings out some of these points when he notes that most experiments in pupil democracy have taken place in private rather than state schools. Private schools, he suggests, are insulated from the scrutiny and pressures which tax-maintained schools are subject to. It is parents that finance private schools, and those who send their children to progressive schools usually do so because they prefer liberal discipline and democratic organisation. Moreover, the small size of most private schools is also a factor in facilitating the organisation of student involvement in school government.

The point that attendance at state schools is largely seen as compulsory and paid for by taxpayers means that head teachers have to be sensitive to the views of the local press, politicians and parents. This may not be a problem if the school council in question is one which can make decisions on only a limited range of matters or which is subject to the head's veto (Ungoed-Thomas, 1972). However, if the council is to have real powers over uniform, smoking, curriculum, discipline, resource allocation, appointments, etc. then, as John Watts (1980) argues, a substantial change is needed in the role of the head. Indeed, because of the political difficulties raised by outside pressures and the need for staff unity, he is doubtful whether an existing school could go over to a participatory approach (Watts, 1977). Knight (1981) tends to confirm this when writing about the failure to provide a fully effective system of student representation at Thomas Bennet School in Crawley, noting that the key problem was that the position of the secondary-school head

made it impossible for any system to be more than marginally successful: 'The autonomy of the Head, and the very wide areas over which he
has virtually untrammelled responsibility, make the transmission of real
powers to the students a virtual impossibility. In such circumstances
consultation is possible but delegation is denied.'

Nevertheless, a thorough and well organised system of consultation
prior to decision-making is preferable to autocracy and can provide a
useful half-way house on the road to fuller participation. At Sidney
Stringer School in Coventry (Open University, 1976), where such a
system has been in operation, the staff seem to have been won over
rapidly to the new methods. Moreover, one observer noted that once
the seeds of participation had been planted there was an increasing
tendency for decisions to be made collectively rather than by a process
of individual consultation.

Another way forward has been suggested by the Campaign for State
Supported Alternative Schools. This group proposes that within the
same geographical area the state should provide real alternatives
between which parents can choose. This would create the finance for
small, non-authoritarian schools where parents send their children by
choice. What is interesting about this suggestion is its combination of
the anti-authoritarianism of much of the left with the right's emphasis on
personal choice. Denmark and Holland already run systems which
provide state finance for such 'independent' schools and after examining
them in practice Rhodes Boyson (1982) concluded that 'Such a system
really would be transferring "power to the people with no increase in
cost to public funds".'

A further objection to the idea of democratic school structures which
is often raised is that the students are too young and immature to
participate in running a school. Research by Connel (1971) and Stevens
(1982) on the political cognitive development of children suggests that
by their early teens children have the necessary conceptual equipment
to understand. What they may lack is the necessary knowledge, skills,
values and experience, and this is what participation helps to teach.
Primarily the problem is how best to organise the induction of students
into the system so that their democratic skills develop with increasing
maturity (Ungoed-Thomas, 1972; Cohen, 1981; and Wilby, 1983).

THE COMMUNITY

If schools are going to pay more than lip-service to the idea of education for democracy in the future they must become more open at the level of the classroom and at the level of the school as a whole. A third consideration in regard to the openness of the school is the extent to which the school and the community permeate each other. One obvious way in which this can be beneficial to political education is by regularly either bringing those involved in the political process (councillors, MPs, magistrates, police, etc.) into the school or taking pupils out to meet them. The former is often preferable if student skills of questioning and argument are to be developed, because students are less shy on their home ground and classes can be primed on background and possible questions beforehand. Handled well, a rigorous questioning session can be very educational for students.

A second way in which the school might enrich the political education of its students in the future has been suggested by Keith Webb (1980). He argues that schools could arrange for students to be involved in voluntary groups outside the school; these would be groups such as the Disablement Income Group, MIND, Shelter, etc., rather than overtly ideological groups. Such placements would be developed in the context of professional/vocational experience within social and general studies courses. The feasibility of the idea therefore comes from the instrumental rather than the ideological nature of the goals of the groups with which the students would work. Nevertheless, these groups are by their very nature involved in political pressure, so at the same time as getting experience of working with the mentally handicapped or the homeless, students would be able to observe and participate in political action at first hand. The teaching of politics in the school would be concurrent, so that theory and practice are discussed. Although Webb notes that such a scheme is 'yet to be demonstrated practicable in the school context', he concludes that 'There seems no good reason why, if politics is to be part of the curriculum, the same principle should not be applied as that underlying field studies in geography'.

CONCLUSION

In a democracy suffrage isn't enough: citizens should also have the right, when necessary, to influence more directly decisions on matters such as housing, education, roads, etc. which affect their lives. These decisions may be of the sort made by central and local government or by institutions of which they are members. The right to have some say in such decisions may involve pressure-group activity and work in committees. Such a right, however, means little unless citizens have the knowledge and skills to put the right into practice. Political power is not evenly distributed in our society, and there is much that the state sector could do to provide the political knowledge and skills that would go some way to redressing the balance.

REFERENCES

Allen, G. (undated) *Researching Political Education — the work of PERU*, unpublished, obtainable from the Department of Education, University of York.

Blumler, J. (1974) Does political ignorance matter?, *Teaching Politics*, 3 (2).

Bowles, S. and Gintis, H. (1976) *Schooling in Capitalist America*. London: Routledge & Kegan Paul.

Boyson, R. (1982) Going Dutch to give power to the parents, *Guardian*, 23 August.

Brennan, T. (1981) *Political Education and Democracy*, Chapter 2. Cambridge: Cambridge University Press.

Bridges, D. (1979) *Education, Democracy and Discussion*. Windsor: NFER.

Cohen, L. (1981) Political literacy and the primary school, *Teaching Politics*, 10 (3).

Connel, R. (1971) *The Child's Construction of Politics*. Melbourne: Melbourne University Press.

Ehman, L. (1977) *The Function of the School in the Political Socialisation Process*, prepared for the International Conference on Political Socialisation and Political Education in Tutzing, West Germany.

Entwistle, H. (1971) *Political Education in a Democracy*. London: Routledge & Kegan Paul.

Guardian (1982) Work is no longer even mentioned as an option, 19 October.

Harber, C. (1983) Assessing political skills, *Teaching Politics*, 12 (2).

Knight, J. (1981) Thomas Bennet rules, in Bailey, T. and Renner, G., *Education for Democracy in Comprehensive Schools in Europe*. Berlin: Institute for European Teacher Education.

Kohl, H. (1970) *The Open Classroom*. London: Methuen.

Lister, I. (1982) Why is civic education necessary?, *International Journal of Political Education*, 5 (3).

Open University (1976) *A Case-study in Management: Sidney Stringer School and Community College*. Milton Keynes: Open University Press.

Porter, A. (1979) The programme for political education, *Social Science Teacher*, 8 (3).

Sarup, M. (1982) *Education, State and Crisis*. London: Routledge & Kegan Paul.

Schools Council (1981) *The Practical Curriculum*. London: Methuen.

Schools Cultural Studies Project Handbook No. 4 (undated) *Discussion as a Teaching Strategy*. Education Centre, New University of Ulster.

Selby, D. (1984) World studies: towards a global perspective in the school curriculum, *Social Science Teacher,* **13** (1).

Shipman, M. (1971) *Education and Modernisation.* London: Faber and Faber.

Smith, M. (1981) *Organise.* Leicester: NAYC Publications. Useful for ideas on teaching political skills.

Stacey, B. (1978) *Political Socialisation in Western Society.* London: Edward Arnold. On books for children see Dixon, B. *Catching them Young.* London: Pluto Press.

Stevens, O. (1982) *Children Talking Politics.* Oxford: Martin Robertson.

Stradling, R. (1977) *The Political Awareness of the School Leaver.* London: The Hansard Society.

Thomas, H. (1982) What about the workers?, *Guardian,* 25 September.

Times Educational Supplement (1982) Growing number of schools opting for political education, 28 May.

Ungoed-Thomas, J.R. (1972) *Our School.* Harlow: Longman. An account of limited school democracy.

Virgo, P. (1982) New work for old, *Guardian,* 26 October.

Watts, J. (1977) *The Countesthorpe Experience.* Hemel Hempstead: George Allen and Unwin.

Watts, J. (1980) *Towards an Open School.* Harlow: Longman.

Webb, K. (1980) Political education through action: a practical strategy for schools?, *Teaching Politics,* **9** (2).

White, B. (1976/77) *School Without Walls* pack, can be obtained from Bob White, 42 Clifton Gardens, London W9.

White, P. (1979) Workplace democracy and political education, *Journal of Philosophy of Education,* **13**.

Whitty, G. and Young, M. (1976) *Explorations in the Politics of School Knowledge.* Nafferton: Nafferton Books.

Wilby, P. (1983) The ruling classes learn to have a say, *Sunday Times,* 8 May.

World Studies Project (1979) *Learning for Change in World Society.* London: One World Trust.

5

The changed role of the classroom teacher

John Watts

INTRODUCTION

We do not need a crystal ball to discover what changes schools have to accommodate. In this respect 'the future is now', to quote Alvin Toffler. The educational system has always displayed great inertia, a built-in resistance to change, which is contributed to by teachers and parents alike. Teachers, enjoying tenure, will resist any radical departure from the attitudes and practices they acquired in initial training and, more particularly, during probation: nobody wants their own established expertise threatened. Parents, on the other hand, however much they have suffered at school or even if they left it with a sense of failure, usually attribute the shortcomings to themselves rather than to the system, and thus find it difficult to envisage school in any form other than the one that they themselves experienced during youth, with consequent suspicion of innovation in school; they are wary of what might seem to jeopardise their children's chances.

So we tend to provide the schooling that was appropriate for an earlier generation. This might have mattered little in an age of prolonged stability, but our age is unique in the pace at which change, with its 'accelerative thrust', has been occurring. Some of the changes already well established in society are irresistably forcing themselves upon schools; others are clear enough for us to see what effect they will continue to have as new patterns emerge. I propose to examine briefly a few manifestations of change in their effect on the classroom teacher. The resulting profile portrays a teacher who is going to either suffer a considerable degree of stress or enjoy an exciting and satisfying professional life, depending on attitude and temperament. Either way, there are important implications for initial and in-service training.

Before taking up the specific points there is need for a few preliminaries. The changes that have already come about can in some instances be attributed to changes in the education system alone. For a start, we have hardly yet come to terms with the progressive raising of the school-leaving age over the period since the end of the Second World War. Many teachers still in harness have seen that age rise from fourteen to fifteen and then to sixteen, and finally there has been the more recent silent raising to seventeen. However gradual this may have appeared, it has still been too rapid for the teachers to accommodate, and attitudes still relate more to the thirteen-year-old schoolchild than to a sixteen-year-old school student. Major things happen to the adolescent over that short age gap, and teachers have adjustments to make. Such development has occurred alongside external changes of enormous import, foremost among which may be placed the explosion of knowledge, the decline in recognition of authority, increased social mobility, moral pluralism and multiculturalism. All these modifications in society present the teacher with a vastly altered task. Although these changes may be regretted or resented, there is little teachers can do to resist them. It is not impossible, however, that without sacrifice of their values they can recognise and respond to them.

ATTITUDES TO AUTHORITY

Less deferential attitudes of the general public towards conventional authority figures are not all that new, and certainly do not stem from the slackening of discipline in schools, as some right-wing politicians would claim. They may well have their origins in the disillusion with leadership that followed the terrible massacres of the First World War; they may have various causes. But whether we like it or not, schoolchildren are far less ready to do what they are told. They want justifications for what they are asked to do. This may be irksome for their teachers, but there is no escaping the fact that explanations of purpose are more necessary than ever before, especially when the options and variety within the curriculum are so numerous. The rituals of school, by which values were transmitted without the need for explanation or justification, no longer carry the magic they once did. The students will ask, 'What are we meant to be doing this for?'. Morning assembly in most secondary schools is a clear example. Rituals, once emptied of their power to carry conviction, become counterproductive. So the teachers on any school staff, both individually and collectively, need to have clear objectives and be able and willing to make those objectives known to their students. It is no longer acceptable to be told 'Do this and it will (somehow or other) be good for you, if not now, then in the long run'. The student in this day of urgency wants to see the pay-off now. There are implications in this for school rules. Every school, like any society, needs some clear rules, some statement of social and academic standards. But, as with the law, the subjects need to see the justice of them, to be free to argue about their interpretation and to feel that they are open to modification. What is more, in schools where the age limit has steadily risen, the students need to know that the rule is one to which teachers are subject jointly with the students. This may sound acceptable when the rule is against running along corridors, but raises some awkward complexities when applied, say, to items of dress and adornment. The demand is for the teacher to observe increased mutuality and be ready with more explicit justifications for the demands made upon students.

BEYOND INSTRUCTION

The growth of knowledge, not only in every existing field, but in a rapidly increasing number of new fields, means that even within the secondary school there can be no certainty that any selection from that sum total will correspond to what the students will find relevant to their life and work in ten or twenty years' time. How many maths teachers, when training, prepared for the use of computers with eleven-year-olds? How many science teachers have had to learn recently about the principles and practices of laser technology? Increasingly, as part of this mutuality, the teacher has had to become a learner. Gone are the days when the teacher had to maintain the myth that one head could hold all necessary knowledge. No longer is the teacher the fountain of all wisdom. In a rapidly changing environment, the teacher is often setting out with the students upon discovery and experiment. Nevertheless, the teacher remains the principal resource, the obvious agent in the learning business for the student. The teacher may not be expected always to have the answer, but remains the expert in the means of arriving at that answer. The teacher has become even more clearly 'the expert learner'. The teacher is the one who knows the range of techniques appropriate to a given situation, who knows where other materials and equipment are available, who knows how to retrieve information that will otherwise remain locked away. The teacher is still the key-holder to knowledge. How important it is, then, that the teacher remains accessible to the student. Traditionally the teacher was the 'possessor' of knowledge and could dispense it to the students in a sort of bargaining game. As the 'key-holder' it would still be possible to play that game, of course, but there is less satisfaction for the teacher in playing it. As the agent rather than the instructor, the teacher has the satisfaction of directing the student's footsteps, without necessarily being there to hand out the answers. As I shall go on to say a little later, the teacher will increasingly be engaged in a dialogue about the learning process, and it is for this reason that the student needs to feel that there is easy access to the teacher. If learning resources are confined less and less to the classroom, then the teacher needs to be available in other places. This is not to argue that morning, noon and night the teacher should have no peace and freedom from work, but it may challenge the habit of teachers of shutting themselves off in staffrooms for most of their non-teaching time, or hedging themselves round by rituals that make it difficult for all but the most skilful to get what they want out of them.

Not only will the teacher be less certain of what needs to be learned, other than what someone else (some other teacher) has written into the syllabus, but the process of learning will often be more significant than any answers that result from it. The very uncertainty of the future and the prevalence of change in all walks of life have rendered the ability to learn more valuable, more conducive to survival and prosperity, than memorised information. Consequently the teacher is often in the position of negotiating with the students, not only about which of the options of their syllabus they should choose to take, but about what the strategies of study and the possible learning outcomes might be. An example of this would be where a teacher of social studies has agreed with a student that she will make a study of local housing development as a part of a course in urban studies. The teacher is particularly interested in the decline of local agriculture, and asks the student to map any housing estates built in the last ten years and draw conclusions about the erosion of farming land by the building of these estates. The student agrees to carry out the mapping exercise, but explains that what she is interested in is not the erosion of agriculture but the cause of urban mobility. She wants to interview a selection of householders on these new estates to find out their reasons for having come to live there. The initial task will be agreed, but the objectives will be different and the conclusions will be drawn in a totally different area. What is the teacher to do? Surely, negotiate. Alas, our traditions run counter to negotiation. We have always been, as Goethe put it, either the hammer or the anvil. And yet how much more analogous to real-life working situations is the spirit of negotiation. Of course, this implies a one-to-one relationship between the teacher and the student that is not possible when direction is being given to a whole class. But there are means and techniques which can make a round of individual or small-group negotiations perfectly feasible. (For a good, practical account of working like this with 14 to 16-year-olds in a comprehensive school, see Martin, R. and Smith, J. A case for conversation, in Haigh (1979).)

EMERGING FROM THE SHELTER OF SPECIALISM

What has been suggested so far already presents a threat to the recognised internal boundaries. Take subjects, for example: the freedom to negotiate the outcomes of study permits the student who has engaged to work with a teacher of rural science to come up with findings in the domain of the teacher of sociology. The teacher will not only need to be on working terms with colleagues in other subjects, but will have to endure the stress of never knowing where the work will lead. This uncertainty may be stimulating at times, but there is no denying that over a period of time it becomes wearing. The uncertainty factor, however, is inescapable. It will extend to the structure of the curriculum, which as never before will be under running review, if not within the school then in public debate. There seems no reason why the teacher should be exempt from this peculiar hazard of living in the late twentieth century, but it does mean that teaching cannot be the safe refuge from the hurly-burly that some once thought it could be. For the head teacher there is even more reason to face the stress of conflict and debate instead of hoping one day to have got the curriculum and timetable about right and be able to lean back at last. The head can no longer hope to sweep conflict among staff under the carpet. However, conflict may be seen as a means of generating positive debate, of arriving at consensus and, as a result, achieving commitment of staff to the policies and practices that result in the process. A staff barred from open consideration of its conflicts will seldom be the 'happy staff' that head teachers used to yearn for: more often such a staff will simply rumble with unexpressed resentments and rivalries instead of finding a coherence in shared purpose.

The model of conflict offered, leading through negotiated compromise to consensus, coherence and commitment, is itself a major threat to cherished classroom and departmental autonomy. It suggests that certain practices may have to be sacrificed for the greater good of such things as an intelligible curriculum or a meaningful system of recording and reporting. It exemplifies the degree to which teachers are being expected to forgo their professional independence in the classroom. There was a time when a teacher, spurs having been won, could organise the classroom as he or she wanted and teach in a personally satisfying, perhaps eccentric and idiosyncratic style, as long as nobody else's prerogatives were infringed and parents did not complain. The tendency has been for greater unity within departments or faculties, or across disciplines in curriculum teams. In these circumstances, individual style may have to be modified in the cause of team coherence. In this, of course, the teacher is being asked to do only what is required in most other walks of life, where working in teams has long been the normal style. It is ironic, though, in a profession which traditionally has put so much emphasis on the team spirit, that its members should find it so hard to abide by it themselves. However, the teacher is not being forced to give up classroom autonomy for continued isolation under someone else's direction; the trade-off should be that each member of the staff may have a greater say in the forging of a group style and an acceptable curriculum. Head teachers need to recognise this *quid pro quo*.

If the teacher is being coaxed out of the shelter of specialism, being urged to become more of a learner, then the range of available strategies for learning has to be increased. The teacher has to become increasingly resourceful. For a start this entails knowing what is available in the school as a whole, what is in the resource centre, the library, and the minds and cupboards of colleagues in other departments. The teacher has to become more sociable within the school. There is no place left for the workshop master who let himself in each morning and sat dragonlike on his board all day, making his tea over the forge and pleading devotion to his tools and to his subject. The student will be moving about, taking what is to be had from every possible source, and if teachers are to be useful in guidance through that maze, they will need to have threaded it themselves. What is more, there is growing recognition of the fact that no school has contained within its walls all the resources for learning: the teacher needs to be conversant not only with what there is to hand but also with what lies within reach outside the institution. What are the national repositories? Who has videos available for school hire? Which companies will lend equipment? Where is it possible to send students for a day's experience in local industry or commerce? In other words, the teacher needs to know the field of work experience. In addition, there is evidence of how often a school will have within ten minutes' walk of its gates, experience, skill and goodwill, on tap from members of the local community, waiting to

be used and glad to feel useful. (The Community Education Development Centre at Coventry has run an interesting project to encourage
such community exploitation.) There will be considerable advantage to
the teacher who has systematically stored information about what is
known and available locally; and it is worth realising that nothing
arouses so much support for an institution as feeling that you are being
of use to it.

In all these considerations, subject boundaries form a very limiting
straitjacket that any enterprising teacher will quickly want to shed. This
kind of exploratory approach inevitably spreads itself across the curriculum: this not only will mean greater likelihood of students realising that
knowledge is interrelated, but it accords with the advice of Her
Majesty's Inspectorate. In their *Aspects of Secondary Education in
England* (DES, 1979) they reported:

> Many schools were aware that a curriculum made up of individual
> subjects, however carefully chosen to provide a balanced pro-
> gramme, may not necessarily result in a coherent experience for the
> pupils or provide all the opportunities they need.

Also:

> There is the risk, in the absence of cooperative, coherent planning,
> that some pupils' programmes will be made up of subjects which
> duplicate certain experiences and ways of thinking (no bad thing in
> itself but often unexploited because the overlap was unplanned) and
> leave out other skills and experiences.

So this is no call for a rag-bag curriculum, but rather for a co-ordinated,
inter-disciplinary register of resources inside and outside the school
which is familiar to all staff and used by them in collaboration with each
other.

In looking over the boundary walls in so many ways, particularly in
looking to the local community as a resource for learning, the teacher
will be brought into increased contact with the world of work and
self-employment. The isolation of school from the realities of the
community, in and out of work, has been notorious, and to some degree
has been the cause of recent major initiatives from outside the education
service. The MSC has started to provide what the public has failed to
find, or even accept as a potential, within the education service. The
breach is most likely to be healed by schools opening their doors to a
genuine two-way movement. Community education is not a new idea,
but for too long it has been thought of as a one-way affair, with the
facilities of the school being made available to the public. We are still a
long way, however, from a reciprocity of services and complementing of
school programmes with studies out of school, whether linked with FE

or making use of training facilities in commerce and industry. There is also hope that such openness would provide at least a more fruitful context for a re-examination of the meaning of work, for exploring afresh the concepts of occupation, creativity, community contribution and work. There is also much hope in the removal of the myth, too long clung to by teachers, that more work for examinations leads to better qualifications, increased success in employment and a generally improved life-style. That threadbare notion must be replaced, and there is a lot of rethinking to be done as a result.

Can the teacher bear all this increased responsibility? Not alone. That is the key to the problem. Without collaboration and openness the teacher will find the burden intolerable; with a renewed professionalism, one that welcomes reciprocal relationships with students and partnership within the community, the teacher will find a new identity. This may seem idealistic, but nothing less is needed, unless schools are to become our social dodos. The sharing of problems by teachers in a school and the refusal to pass the buck up the line of the hierarchy mean added demand upon time and energy. But in the long run it also means greater professional pay-off, a greater dignity on the part of teachers, who would have a major part in the shaping of the policies and the working detail of teaching life rather than remaining just the bottom-rung exponents of a private craft whose constraints and resources are determined by others. I have specified elsewhere in greater detail the kind of 'new covenant' that this would require (Watts, 1980). The relationships proposed are not outlandish; they have been made to work productively and harmoniously, but so far only in isolated pockets. A real alternative within the maintained system of schooling is possible, economically viable, and overdue.

CONCLUSION

This chapter has attempted to describe the changes that have been taking place in the role of the teacher. The changes have occurred in the practice of teachers themselves at certain points in the life of schools in a way that may appear to be scattered but which amounts to a distinct organic development. At the same time, the external changes are such that the teaching role variations need to become more widespread, and to that extent this chapter is also a tract urging those who are dragging their feet to listen to what has been going on in the schools and in society as a whole, and to bring themselves up to date. Such is the impatience of some who have watched the slow progress of education in a rapidly changing milieu, notably industry and the Ministry of Employment, that chunks of the educational process are being taken over by non-educationalists. It is no use teachers just holding up their hands in horror: they must meet the challenge.

Perhaps the greatest single factor in determining whether the necessary changes come about will be in-service programmes for teachers and head teachers. The trouble here is that so much of the INSET provision operates on a deficiency model, offering piecemeal remedial courses for teachers on the supposition that they, or someone advising them, have identified a specific deficiency that the course will put right. It is a method analogous to having a car serviced. This may be of use while the overall pattern of teaching is acceptable, but we are at a stage where the model needs a new design. Programmes of in-service training should enable teachers to take a total view of their role and function, and confront them with the awkward questions of what they are supposed to be doing and whether they could do it any better. Such a holistic basis to in-service work requires two things which are hard to come by and which LEAs and head teachers need to be more generous about: time and hospitality. Time is needed because qualitative shifts in attitude will come about only when teachers and trainers have had enough of each other's company and inquiry to develop trust and frankness. The other commodity, hospitality, entails teachers opening their classrooms to each other for pooled comment and support. The changes are going to be painful in many cases and require far more support than is normally given to teachers. Unsupported, they will resist change and criticism. With help, particularly from their peers and their head teachers, the thaw may begin.

What is being asked for, in brief, is an application of the same principles of mutuality, negotiation, speculation and constructive evaluation at the level of teacher education as are being urged here between the teacher and the student. To be consistent, it seems only obvious that the two levels should reflect each other in this way.

REFERENCES

DES (1979) *Aspects of Secondary Education in England.* London: HMSO.
Haigh, G. (ed.) (1979) *On Our Side.* London: Maurice Temple Smith.
Watts, J.F. (1980) *Towards an Open School.* Harlow: Longman.

6

Alternatives in education from the Third World

Lynn Davies

INTRODUCTION

An apt and telling strip cartoon in a book on education in developing countries depicts a hand throwing a lifebelt to a large group of people drowning in the sea after a shipwreck. There is a struggle for the belt, and as the one victor swims to safety on it (and the rest perish), the hands of the thrower are seen applauding him (Ottoson, 1978). Such an illustration represents the growing realisation among many Third World countries of the absurdity of an education system that rewards only a few. Many 'poor' countries inherited a colonial system of education, often British; from their struggles for independence they are recognising not only the 'irrelevance' of such styles of schooling to their culture and economy, but that competitive, academic education can be directly harmful to goals of national unity and full utilisation of labour. In many ways, developing countries can see the inherent weaknesses in Western systems of education more clearly than Western countries can, and a curious reversal is appearing. Not only can the UK no longer be seen as the provider of 'expert' educational aid to the Third World, but the UK itself, with high unemployment and a stagnating economy, may be viewed increasingly as an underdeveloped country. In our appraisal of 'what went wrong' and of the contribution of schooling to our decline, we are in a position to learn from both the 'successes' and the 'mistakes' of alternative educational strategies in so-called developing societies.

Although there are, of course, a host of complementary and competing models, three linked themes might be taken as being particularly relevant to the UK: education for self-reliance, education with production, and functional literacy. Underpinning all is the old notion that human capital is the most important resource a nation has, yet realising that human potential should not be viewed as an individualised identification of 'talent' for the formation of new elites, but as the means to co-operative grassroots enterprises.

This chapter will draw on ideas from various parts of Africa as well as from Papua New Guinea and Cuba, in arguing the need to learn from others' attempts at alternatives. The immediate problem of 'translation' must be admitted at the outset. Just as the direct importation of colonial systems was often antithetical to local needs, alternative educational strategies based on the requirements of largely rural economies would seem at first sight to have little relevance to inner-city comprehensives in the UK. We do not have the problems of the drift away from the countryside, of massive illiteracy (or do we?) or of teacher shortages (quite the reverse). In an already 'high tech', mechanised and computerised society, we have no need to encourage people back to the fields; with cars produced by robots, the notion of an intermediate technology based on labour-intensive, small-scale methods would seem an anachronism. However, this chapter will argue that our schools and their personnel also appear to be produced by robots, and that an underlying principle of self-determination in education and employment should be common to all peoples. The core problems that bedevil new approaches in education in the developing world are the same ones that undermine radical initiatives in the UK: the divide between mental and manual, between academic and practical; the demand for assessment and certification, with its resultant qualification inflation; and the desire by individuals and groups to use education as a means of upward mobility or of maintaining elite status. Unfortunately, we may be able to learn more from why some projects fail in the Third World than we can from the apparent successes, for the failures may be seen to stem not necessarily from the 'poverty' of a country, from lack of material or pedagogical resources, but from the attempt to change schooling without simultaneously being able to revolutionise employment opportunities or existing hierarchies in the world of work or family. Yet this does not mean that shifts in educational thinking are without import, and the successes also have much to teach us, much to make us feel uneasy about in our assumptions about 'good' educational practice.

EDUCATION FOR SELF-RELIANCE

While now widely discussed, the main example of education for self-reliance has been Tanzania, based on Nyerere's educational philosophy, ujamaa, or socialism. Primary and secondary schools were not to be seen simply as academic preparation for further studies, but as an integral part of the community and a preparation for life and service in the village and the rural economy. Students and parents were to be involved in decision-making, and authoritarian teaching methods and control were to give way to democratic community responsibility. With primary schools offering self-contained courses and secondary schools ceasing to be merely a selection process for higher education, students were to be made aware of the obligation to use expensive education to serve the mass of the people. Exams were to be downgraded in Government and public esteem, and combined with teachers' assessments of 'character' and 'willingness to serve' in terms of school and community work. The schools were to teach self-reliance by *being* self-reliant — growing their own vegetables, maintaining buildings, raising poultry and cattle, and participating in self-help projects in the community.

Tanzania's initiatives have faltered in some areas because of inadequate preparation of teachers to relinquish an authoritarian role, but also because of the difficulty of educating people to forgo status based on written qualifications. Teachers, as Adams (1981) discovered, were still expected to:

> nurture, examine and select the few for advancement (at the primary and secondary levels) while at the same time to extol the virtues of working and living on the land to the vast majority of their students. The new philosophy appears to have presented an inherently contradictory view of the teacher's role. In addition, like the bureaucrats, their own educational experiences in terms of academic success, selection and promotion leading to secure wage employment would tend inevitably to reinforce the former role and relegate the latter to 'extra-curricular activities'.

Neither would parents necessarily accept the 'complete cycle' approach of primary education, wanting it to lead on to further opportunities, while the vocational implications of self-reliance would appease them only if matched by employment prospects in the rural areas.

Part of the problem has been the attempt to implement self-reliance methods across the whole country simultaneously. Other countries have chosen to start with pilot schools, or to use a step-wise approach to educational change. An initiative based on a similar philosophy to Nyerere's is that of the 'youth village' in the Seychelles, which is to replace traditional secondary schooling. Volunteer teenagers in three areas have been given the task of building a self-reliant village, producing their own food and their own energy, building their own radio station and deriving their own culture. Formal teaching has been largely abandoned, and instead teachers are attached to working 'blocs' and co-operatives, explaining radio waves to the broadcaster, or marine biology to the fishing group. Mental and manual work co-exist. Boys have learned to cook and clean; girls muck out the pigsties and learn construction. They are, for President René, 'the seeds of the new society', who when they leave will institute centres of socialist initiative in the country as a whole (Le Brun, 1982). The aim is to build up areas of socialist relations which will gradually join up and expand. Workers' organisations and political involvement have been strengthened simultaneously, with all wage workers now in trade unions. The recently attempted coup in the Seychelles demonstrates, however, the ability of the old commercial and landed interests to organise themselves to maintain political and cultural power, and to enlist South African help.

Although the end product of a 'self-reliant' individual would appear to be non-controversial and not particularly radical (indeed it might seem in line with current Conservative ideology of 'responsibility' and pulling oneself up by one's bootstraps) the resistances to, and difficulties with, the African initiatives show that the philosophy potentially has a revolutionary force. There is a difference between education for self-reliance and education for subsistence. Groups who are self-reliant aim at not continuously needing experts to tell them what to do, or needing certificates telling the world they can do it, or having the profits of their labour siphoned off elsewhere. That this is threatening to established educational and occupational interests is self-evident: the notion of selective self-reliance is a contradiction in terms, for the educational process aims at the whole community, not just the 'able' or 'bright'. This implies redefining concepts of 'ability'. (For a fuller discussion of this see Davies, 1980.) One cannot have a bottom tier of 'self-reliant' people if others are still taking decisions for them. Any moves towards education for self-reliance in the UK would have to examine very carefully the question of entrenched interests in the academic qualification spiral.

One attempt to balance the interests of self-reliance and formal assessment is Papua New Guinea's Secondary Schools Community Extension Project (SSCEP). Here the school curriculum has been redesigned to integrate the practical and the intellectual; formal assessment is skill-based, linked to project work in the community. The students spend periods of time at 'outstations' where they, with the teachers, must participate in the solving of community problems. The primary aim of the outstations is educational, not economic; the students are not to become cheap labour, even though the outstations aim at becoming self-supporting. The interesting feature of SSCEP is the *systematic* integration of the vocational and the academic. In Tanzania, teachers sometimes interpreted self-reliance simply as productive work, which, if anything, impeded the main academic aims of their teaching. The 'character' assessment there tended to become a formality, and academic success was still the accountable and most visible aspect of schools. In the SSCEP project, however, the 'academic' qualification is gained only if the student has demonstrated skill at applying curriculum content to the solution of practical community issues. The SSCEP rationale recognises the powerful motivating force of selection for further education and salaried employment, but hopes to turn the extrinsic motivation of exams into longer-term intrinsic motivation, in that the student learns to find the problem-solving application of school curriculum items a rewarding activity in itself. The 'carrot' of exams 'can be used to develop behaviours which will survive the consumption of the carrot' (McNamara, 1982).

It appears to be not a question of making the practical have 'equal status' with the academic (that was shown to fail as long ago as the tripartite system here) but of making definitions of academic *derive from* the vocational. I used to think that getting rid of the exam orientation of our schools would be as difficult as, say, getting 300 women into Parliament. I now believe I was over-optimistic. If we cannot foresee educational life without exams, then the least we can do is make them criterion-referenced and skill-based, and deny the notion that there can be any useful demonstration of 'pure' theory divorced from the real-life situations that pupils find themselves in.

EDUCATION WITH PRODUCTION

Initiatives around education for self-reliance are clearly linked to the idea of service to the community. Another rationale is the premise that all people need intrinsic job satisfaction, yet with automation and rising unemployment this becomes increasingly difficult within the formal economy. It has been predicted, for example, that the UK will need only 10 per cent of today's labour force to supply all its material needs by AD 2010 (Stonier, 1978). Third World countries, of course, cannot afford luxuries such as 'education for leisure', and in general have not been sidetracked down such sterile and potentially socially divisive paths. Instead there are initiatives such as the Foundation for Education with Production (FEP), which has more to do with the idea that self-determination comes from the possession of capabilities of social or economic *value*. The FEP, a non-governmental organisation, was set up in 1980 by a group of African educationalists, and now has sections in countries in Europe as well as the Third World. The general aim is to equip people to be in charge of their own lives through work which they control; in this country the direction would be towards self-employment and co-operatives:

> The needs of the market for standardised, mass produced goods will increasingly be met through capital and technology intensive processes. A growing number of firms will be squeezed out of the formal economic system and the pool of structurally unemployed will take on politically dangerous and economically crippling proportions. The only, currently known, constructive alternative to authoritarian measures, e.g. conscription and/or compulsory public-work service, is to stimulate market outlets for high quality, maintainable goods and personalised services, environmental improvements, maintenance, repair and other conservation activities. To be active in this kind of system — currently known as the informal economy — firms and groups of individuals will need to be versatile, self-directing and innovatory. *(Waldmann, 1981)*

Education with production is geared to this self-direction, and claims to have particular school benefits:

> Giving children employable skills, especially the financial management and business skills now almost completely neglected, which are so vital for self-employment.
> Helping to interest and motivate children by involving them in things which are fun to do and lead to a tangible end product. This would be particularly helpful for those older children in countries like the UK who see little chance of success in gaining certificates.
> (especially in developing countries) Contributing towards meeting the costs of the school.
> (especially in developing countries) Helping to make learning more meaningful through practical work and experience, as opposed to the all-too-common situation where the teacher stands in front of the class dictating notes to the pupils. *(Knox and Castles, 1982)*

With regard to the second point, I have already expressed doubts about any dual system which *contrasts* practical competence with certificate-gaining, but the subsequent points about cost contribution and teacher styles may in fact be just as relevant to the UK. It is worth looking at the practical implementations of education with production already in existence to see what lessons can be learned.

The historical background to FEP lies with Patrick von Rensburg and the Serowe Brigades in Botswana in the mid-1960s. In order to meet the problem of the mass of primary-school pushouts whose schooling had equipped them for little of practical value, the brigades were established as production units in activities like farming, building, tanning, forestry, sheet metal work, printing, motor maintenance and carpentry. The trainees spent about 80 per cent of their time on production combined with on-the-job training, and the rest on theoretical training and academic lessons in maths, English, Setswana and development studies. The brigades aimed to provide foci of rural development, and it was hoped they would reduce rural–urban migration through improving living standards and educational opportunities in the countryside. They proved highly successful: by the mid-1970s they existed in most of Botswana's towns and larger villages. Also established was Boiteko (self-help), a network of production groups organised on a co-operative basis. Particularly to help women and older members of the community whose conditions the brigades failed to improve, Boiteko was meant to give income-generating work using local materials and resources to produce useful goods for village people, and to provide child care, literacy teaching and other support activities.

These models provided blueprints for other liberation movements in Zimbabwe, South Africa and Namibia, who all sent cadres for training at Serowe; these in turn helped to develop and sharpen the political ideas of the people in the brigades. Yet in the 1970s the Serowe models ran into difficulties. Knox and Castles give a useful analysis of the pressures: for example, the best trainees of the brigades were being enticed away into the towns; other graduates found it hard to find employment; there were internal conflicts about political aims and management policies; the use of labour-intensive traditional production methods kept productivity in the self-help groups too low to offer reasonable levels of income to members. Yet they did contribute to Botswana's rapid expansion, and FEP is an attempt to learn from and broaden the Serowe experiments. The main lesson is always that educational innovation will fail unless it takes into account the economic and political structures immediately around it.

There are continuing examples of education with production in schools in Africa, notably Zimbabwe and Tanzania; their agricultural and building bias make the models difficult to import directly into the UK. The most immediate lessons can perhaps be drawn from producer co-operatives where members learn skills both of the trade itself and of co-operative management. Knox and Castles describe side by side Tshwarango Enterprises in Botswana and the five co-operatives set up by the West Glamorgan Common Ownership Development Agency. Without going into detail on the projects, it is possible to tease out common concerns and problems whatever part of the world a co-operative is started. A clear advantage is the ownership of the assets, and hence the motivation to maintain the enterprise. Another is the need for continual whole-group meetings which, while making decisions on such matters as possible products, market outlets, delegation of tasks and budget predictions, give group members practice in participation and articulation. Apart from finance, problems derive from the need for a profound change in attitudes in terms of developing initiative, collective responsibility and a willingness to take one's fate into one's own hands. Gaining confidence in one's own ability is crucial, and continuous training and support may be necessary initially, so that members can successfully 'take over' from the development officers.

Nobody is suggesting that Eton and Harrow should be turned into worker co-operatives overnight, but that the identification of the sorts of qualities and skills which will be needed for people to work productively in a largely automated society might go some way towards revolutionising our current curriculum and teaching methods.

FUNCTIONAL LITERACY

Discussion of skills leads directly to the third theme: the definition of 'literacy' which underpins any educational ideology. In this country it tends to be restricted to 'reading and writing', except perhaps for ESN schools where a wider range of survival skills may be taught directly. It is largely due to the work of Paulo Friere, initially in Brazil, that the notion of political literacy has gained currency: this is a literacy which enables an individual to be first of all aware of the hidden values of a community or society, of the ways he or she may be oppressed, and then to have the self-confidence and know-how to seek, with others, solutions to the recognised problems. Friere contrasts education for domestication with education for liberation; the former is a subtle conditioning process in which people are led to accept the conditions in which they find themselves and to believe that there is little to be done about them. Again, being labelled as 'less able' would be an example of domestication. A liberating education, on the other hand, makes people aware of their strengths and assures them that they have power over their destiny. Freire developed the use of 'cultural circles' to promote adult literacy: by means of key words and generative themes, groups of people in similar circumstances share their perceptions of common experiences to learn how these experiences can be represented permanently in the written word. For Friere, literacy must have a purpose, and an immediate pressing context. He is scathing about the bland and anodyne 'reading books' designed by people who have little experience of the realities of subjugated and domesticated others. People must be challenged to go beyond reading and writing and learn how to 'read and re-write the reality' (Friere, 1972).

Not all governments, of course, have been sympathetic to Freire's consciousness-raising ideas; even with a supportive government there may be shifts in direction, as current work using his methods in the Cape Verde islands shows. While the ends for Friere would be participation in decision-making in a democracy, the teachers and the students may tend to concentrate on skills which are easily assessable and immediately recognisable. Personal economic motivations for literacy may predominate over political 'conscientisation'.

I suspect that even the combination of verbal and political literacy may not be enough to satisfy individual motivation and to generate social change. What is required is a broader definition of literacy, to fulfil a range of potential needs. Intermedia, an international organisation concerned with literacy education, suggests that for a person to be functionally literate, he or she should be able to cover a six-point list of skill areas, ranging from understanding and running a household, to earning a living and participating in the political activities of the community (Ottoson, 1978). An adaptation and extension of the Intermedia list for the UK might look like this:

1. He or she should be able to read official forms and manufacturers' instructions, to write letters requesting finance or information and to understand numerical quantifications such as production costings, interest rates and rent.
2. He or she should have an understanding of the workings of the local community, its industries and facilities, its social composition and its areas of need.
3. He or she should know how to run a household, including family health, house and clothing repairs, food preparation and budgeting.
4. He or she should have the motivation, knowledge and skills to make a living, *whether or not* jobs are available in the formal economy.
5. He or she should have knowledge of family, housing, employment and consumer law, of welfare benefits, and of the workings of party, union or other organisational political activity; and should have the skills to claim rights and participate politically.
6. He or she should have an image of him or herself as a person who can learn continually, and who in co-operation with others can make decisions and effect change.

This functional literacy will not, of course, come from six bodies of knowledge variously labelled 'number work' or 'social studies'. The link with education for production and self-reliance is that they must be learned by doing them in *real* contexts. In the UK at present there is a dehydration theory of education: that if you give children a sort of dried minestrone package of knowledge, with enough variety in basic dry matter, when reconstituted at any stage in life there will emerge a nourishing soup of whatever flavour desired. The rationale is that you must give children a taste of, for example, geography, in case they like it and want to consume more. The fallacy in the approach is demonstrated not only by the vast amount that we forget irretrievably, but by the anomaly that 'subjects' divorced from their application (together with formal assessment of them) leads to the conviction that there is an option about being able to 'do' them or not. 'I've never been able to do maths' is a statement that arises from never having had to do it to survive. Parents do not say, 'I've never been able to do shopping/child care/meeting relatives': they have learned their skills on the job. But schools breed what Dore terms an 'employee orientation': training people to become part of, and to fit into, large organisations — school, government department or firm. They passively receive instructions from bosses as they have passively received instructions from teachers; they assume that all initiative should come from above, and allow their self-esteem to be determined by external measurements of their own performance rather than developing their own internal, self-reliant standards (Dore, 1973). That this 'employee orientation' is not even always functional is effectively demonstrated by Little's research (Little, 1980) on the correlation between amount of education and productivity: data from all over the world show that differences in educational level appear to be unrelated to supervisors' ratings of individual productivity among groups of people doing the same job. Going to 'conventional' school for longer does not make people more productive. We might learn the lesson that women's self-help groups in developing countries have had to learn (*Journal of Development Studies,* 1981): that only by starting an enterprise do you conceive of the skills and expertise that you need. The women have realised the need for education, not in terms of formal schooling for technology or general literacy, but to learn about accounting, about bank loans and credit schemes, and about how to assert themselves, communicate and articulate ideas. In this they have seriously questioned the whole pattern of educational development aid to date — as well as its gender distribution.

The combined message of the philosophies of education for self-reliance, education with production and functional literacy is, then, far stronger than the old 'education for capability' schemes, for it is extra-institutional: it is that to be self-supporting and self-determining, people must gain from education the realisation *in non-artificial situations* of the functional skills which enable full economic participation.

THE PRODUCTIVE SCHOOL

This is not another argument for 'relevant' education. Simply making the curriculum 'relevant to society' does little to ease the absurdity of taking children out of the community in order to learn about it. And 'work experience' attachments only reinforce the barrier between school and 'work' instead of integrating mental/manual divisions. Relevance programmes for schools, as Sinclair and Lillis show conclusively and sadly from their comparative analysis, are not an appropriate vehicle for the rectification of social and economic ills. Only in conjunction with real work and extension projects can relevance programmes contribute to development in the environment (Sinclair and Lillis, 1980). Therefore I am not arguing either for an elaboration of the notion of 'community service'. Making pupils 'help' in various social situations may elicit a range of personal skills and empathies, but it does not give pupils experience of taking responsibility for a project *and making it a going concern.*

My position would be anyway that people are basically self-interested: their 'help' for others will be limited unless in the long term there is something in it for them. At the moment most education fosters people's self-interest through competitive individualism; with the combination of qualification spirals and decreasing employment opportunities, schools find this motivation hard to sustain. Interestingly, Cuba's attempt to disband the certification orientation of education in its 'Schools to the Countryside' campaign faced similar problems of motivation: students released from the pressure to work for exams did not automatically turn their energies into socially useful rural work or even political discussion groups; many simply 'lay fallow' (Bowles, 1976).

The answer to pupil motivation and declining budgets for education will be to make schools productive units. The linked aims here are a degree of self-help within the school and pupil co-operatives to engage in productive and remunerated enterprises. With regard to the first, urban schools cannot be self-supporting in terms of food production, but it is curious that we believe that anything up to 2000 able-bodied youngsters cannot, or should not, organise their own meals in terms of buying, preparation and distribution. If they were permitted to aim at a small surplus (shock horror), I suggest the enterprise might be even more attractive. Similarly, tenders put in by pupils for school maintenance and decoration might turn out to be very competitive. (The rights of existing workers and the strengths of trade unions, however, must not be underestimated.) Co-operatives that aim at the world outside school might be in the fields of craft, design and technology, or entertainment, or services to the public. The rationale would be to channel self-interest into the workings of a group, into the basic democratic exercise, and to learn the skills and mistakes of business enterprise in a slightly more sheltered and guided atmosphere than if they were starting from scratch outside.

It must be stressed that this is not an option for the 'less able', while the others continue academic pursuits. We could well learn from Papua New Guinea's non-streamed, skill-based examination system and make school certificates dependent on proven competence in the various aspects of 'productivity'. A detailed proposal might help here: let us borrow Carol Stevens' Parental Involvement Project outlined in this volume. The labour-intensive nature of close work with parents of very young children is clear; while not launching into the initial home contacts, pupils could create a co-operative to produce back-up inexpensive toys and educational materials. They would certainly need eventually to test these in co-operation with parents and their pre-school children; the commercial possibilities would also be worth exploiting. Such a project would involve not only the obvious creative and craft skills, but also the financial/mathematical competencies in costing, budgeting, funding and marketing, as well as in understanding of the number concepts needed for small children. It also clearly develops the social knowledge involved in identifying areas of need in the community as well as the practical aspects of communicating and explaining new ideas to others. The 'assessment' part is, however, less obvious. At present I can see no way round reverting to some form of labelled knowledge area. A member of the co-operative particularly interested in a 'maths' qualification would specialise finally in that side and submit proof of competence in using numerical skills in that human situation. Another might develop an 'urban studies' theme by investigating the spatial patterning and material disparities between groups within the community which generated the perceived need for school involvement in home life. A 'sociology' enthusiast might even want to present a political critique of the whole concept and practice of interventionist strategy. The main insistence is that nobody in the school gets a qualification unless they have demonstrated participation in a 'productive' project, and that even if not claiming expertise across all the skill areas involved, they are able to show appreciation of the *integration* of different types of competence needed to tackle a problem.

Such assessment ties in well with current moves to replace one-off examinations at 16 or 18 with series of graded tests. The numerical skills needed to cost out and run a mobile 'stove-wash' service to homes, for example, would be of a lower 'order' than those employing computer technology to market a new product or game. Pupils setting up a 'law shop' in the school to advise the community on legal, financial and welfare rights might be rewarded by higher levels of certificates in law or accountancy than younger pupils concentrating on improving the take-up of free school meals. If it all sounds complicated to administer, we have to remember that resolving such complications is but one example of the lateral thinking that teachers and pupils will have to do to survive and adapt to new demands. Some schools are of course already breaking new ground, at least on the production side, if not yet the assessment. In one example (*Guardian,* 8 June 1983) a four-week project to help a local dentist led to two pupils and a teacher designing a device to make wheelchairs recline. Having won a national competition, 'there were inquiries from all over the world', and the teacher was able to raise £10 000 capital to leave his job and become managing director of a new company to market the device. If that is not an incentive, I don't know what is.

But the major emphasis on production rather than pure knowledge would be in order to minimise the potentially socially divisive nature of certification. Developing countries have obviously linked production mainly with agricultural and craft work; in the UK a broader definition would be needed to include productivity in everything from music to mathematics, from legal to social services. Foster demonstrated as long ago as 1966 the 'colonial fallacy' in Ghana's attempts to develop vocational rural education while white-collar qualifications and city life were still more attractive options for the upwardly aspiring (Foster, 1966). Productive activity must not be the last resort for the unemployable, but the first aim for the schools of the next century. As Nyerere argued, to take young people out of production by education *while remaining consumers* is a luxury a poor country cannot afford.

SUMMARY

The lessons learned from Third World educational alternatives might provisionally be summarised, then, as follows:

1. Expenditure on selective and competitive exam-oriented education has increasingly low returns to a country.
2. Alternatives that merely expand the opportunities to gain academic certificates create structural unemployment, disaffection and increased disdain for vocational work.

3. Alternatives that expand the vocational sector while retaining an academic entry system to the elite entrench social divisions, maintain artificial mental/manual distinctions and diminish both social responsibility for the elite and entrepreneurial incentive for the majority.
4. Alternatives that seek to abolish exams altogether have difficulties unless other forms of personal motivation are found.
5. More successful to date are those initiatives which employ a step-wise, gradual approach to reform and which try to make assessment dependent on functional competence demonstrable in the community.

Translated into a programme for the UK, a potentially productive school would have to conduct three types of searching:

1. Identify an examining board that will agree to monitor skill-based and collective assessment, and canvass higher education institutions and employers to accept such qualifications.
2. Identify a range of outlets for productive activity, either to meet a gap in local provision or to create a wider demand for a high-quality, labour-intensive product. Whether this is provision of a service or creative endeavour, the thrust would be that it must aim at being economic; children must not see themselves as cheap conscripts (as some of the current MSC/YTS programmes imply) but as apprentices learning the direct value of their labour. If fulfilling a community need or solving a community problem, they must identify possible sources of funding and submit proposals themselves; the objective is neither passive welfare recipients nor the salt-mine mentality. Self-esteem comes from a feeling of integrity and control over events.
3. Identify the range of functional skills and team work involved in running a co-operative. Teachers themselves would clearly need a wider and less dominating role than in simple knowledge transmission. In the long term, what the co-operatives produce, design or serve becomes less important than the expertise gained in group decision-making, delegation and leadership, in banking, loans, credit and interest, in inventiveness, problem-solving and lateral thinking, in the use of strategies, marketing, promotional literature, and in targets, deadlines, goal-getting and responsibility to fellow workers.

The argument for the productive school is not as a training ground for little capitalists, but as a starting point for the co-operative ethic which can channel personal initiative into commitment to others.

REFERENCES

Adams, J. (1981) The contribution of education for self-reliance to manpower development in Tanzania — a critical appraisal, *International Journal of Educational Development*, **1** (2).

Bowles, S. (1976) Cuban education and the revolutionary ideology, in Figueroa, P. and Persaud, G. *Sociology of Education: A Caribbean Reader.* Oxford: Oxford University Press.

Davies, L. (1980) The social construction of low achievement, *Educational Review* Special Edition, *Helping the Low Achiever in the Secondary School.*

Dore, R. (1973) Pre-vocational studies: a comment on recent developments in Ceylonese education, *Institute of Development Studies,* discussion paper.

Foster, P. (1966) Vocational school fallacy in development planning, in Anderson, C. and Bowman, M., *Education and Economic Development.* New York: Aldine.

Friere, P. (1972) *Pedagogy of the Oppressed.* Harmondsworth: Penguin.

Journal of Development Studies (1981) Special issue on African Women in the Development Process, **17** (3), April.

Knox, D. and Castles, S. (1982) Education with production — learning from the Third World, *International Journal of Educational Development*, **2** (1).

Le Brun, O. (1982) René's revolution, *Guardian Third World Review*, 19 February.

Little, A. (1980) Is education related to productivity?, *Selection for Employment versus Education,* Institute of Development Studies Bulletin, May.

McNamara, V. (1982) The long-term effect of 'carrots': the secondary school extension project in Papua New Guinea, *International Journal of Educational Development*, **1** (3).

Ottoson, K. (1978) *Thinking about Education.* Guildford: Lutterworth.

Sinclair, M. and Lillis, K. (1980) *School and Community in the Third World.* London: Croom Helm.

Stonier, T. (1978) *Guardian,* 14 November, quoted in Laurie, P. (1980) *The Micro Revolution.* London: Futura.

Waldmann, P. (1981) Learning to be versatile at work, *Journal of European Industrial Training*, **5** (3).

7

Contributions past, present and future, of psychology to education

Brian Roberts

INTRODUCTION

The relationship of psychology to education, from the beginnings of psychology just over 100 years ago (at the time education in parts of the Western world became compulsory), has been an uneasy one, a protracted engagement with few mutual encouragements to wedlock. Teachers and administrators of education alike have been dubious of the theories and empirical findings of psychologists, while the latter have, perhaps, reacted with some exasperation when educators have not shown more willingness to put new ideas into practice. At the time the doom-monger writers of the Black Papers (Cox and Dyson, 1969, 1972) were castigating both camps for falling standards, overall improved results in core areas such as reading, and in the number of 'O'-level and 'A'-level passes gained, were being reported. But no-one claimed that the applications of psychology to education had anything to do with these advances.

From the beginnings of psychology the new science saw itself as having a special pertinence to education. In directing its attention and effort to studying the development of children by observation and experiment, to investigating the processes of learning and the nature of 'intelligence', 'motivation' and 'personality' in children, psychology apparently had easy targets: in contrast to adults, children can easily be observed and experimented on in natural and captive settings — hence the daily diaries of Darwin, Stern and Guillaume and the even closer observations of Piaget. Moreover, as 'the father of the man', the child is seen as illustrating the start and the most rapid stage of the development of human processes. Some theories of behaviour, especially those modelling learning processes and psychoanalysis, have appeared so compellingly relevant to the development of children and to education that schools were created to apply and demonstrate the advantages of the new ideas. Montessori in Holland and England, The Malting House School in Cambridge, Anna Freud's wartime nursery in Hampstead, The Mulberry Bush School, Bertrand Russell's school at Beacon Hill, and Neill's Summerhill all represented various kinds of scientific approach to the educational and social upbringing of children. Each of them is recorded in some way, and there is even a description, both wry and sad, of what it was like to be on the receiving end of Russell's Watsonian behaviourist approach, by his daughter. Some of these schools still flourish and are seen as essential components of education, for instance The Mulberry Bush School in its psychodynamic treatment of maladjusted children (Dockar Drysdale, 1968), while others on temporary funding or for other reasons disappeared.

Yet it should now be asked, in the face of manifest advances in education, from the rigid information-absorption model and drill-method teaching routines of the Victorian classroom to the multifarious methods of today, if psychology's contributions in both general and specific ways *are* related to this progress. Specifically, one would like to know if they have led to more effective and rewarding learning, if teachers now feel more secure in their understanding of children's behaviour and, perhaps most important, if children more so than in Shakespeare's day creep at faster than a snail's pace and willingly to school. There are, of course, no easy answers to such questions. An unqualified 'yes' to them is unlikely from any of the participants in education, though psychologists can validly point to substantial advances in our understanding of child development and learning processes. I shall focus on some of these areas later, but first I shall examine the problems psychology faces in producing any clear-cut strategies which would dramatically change education into a far more satisfying and successful enterprise.

FORMULATING THE PROBLEMS

Education today faces more problems simultaneously than it has ever done in the past. Recent world-wide reductions in educational spending, a lack of clear teaching and curricular objectives in relation to educational means and ends, a consequent puzzlement about how best to train teachers and head teachers, increasingly voiced dissatisfactions of parents, bored and alienated children in secondary education — all suggest that a quite substantial rethinking of the issues is overdue. The future roles of psychological theory, research and practice will be considered in the final section, but here I would like to elaborate briefly on how psychology apparently has not done very well in aiding our understanding of children in their learning and relationships and therefore might be seen as adding little to more effective education.

There are three main interrelated problems. First, inasmuch as humans have a massively complex system of interacting electrochemical networks, these interacting with quite different kinds of environments (for instance differences in parent handling of a child) at different times of development, behaviour is frequently mystifying and thus seen as unpredictable. Second, because we can't look into the engine of behaviour, the brain, until its moving parts have stopped, we attempt to make inferences about behaviour from observation and from listening to what people say, and both these bases for inference are unreliable for both obvious and more complex reasons. Third, and most important for child, parent and teacher alike, psychologists, like everyone else, have great difficulty in creating theories which satisfactorily and sufficiently explain most, if not all, behaviours, and which 'anchor' our observations and interpretations in such a way as to integrate and make meaningful the behaviour of others and ourselves. (The one thing which is worse than failing to make sense of the behaviour of others is failing to make sense of our own behaviour, as a number of psychologists have pointed out.)

THE CAR-DRIVING PROBLEM

A metaphor will illustrate the above points nicely. A car driver, encased in moving metal, is cut off from direct verbal communication with those outside (unless he or she has two-way radio). The driver also lacks information about the abilities, skills and concentration that other road-users possess at a time when this might be vital. Thus he or she has to make predictions about their behaviour from a very limited range of non-verbal signals, such as the flashing lights and movements of other vehicles. An incorrect signal or ambiguous movement by the car in front 'throws' the driver's anticipations and if there is shortage of time, or lack of concentration on the driver's part, he or she will compound the other driver's errors. Similarly the teacher, the child and the parent (and the psychologist) have difficulty in 'reading' the behaviour of others, in understanding the limits of the resources that people bring to the situations they find themselves in; they resort to inadequate explanations of why someone is behaving in a certain way, and as a consequence respond inadequately. The 'signals' we send to other people, verbal and non-verbal, are often insubstantial and ambiguous, and it is not surprising that children misunderstand parents, teachers misunderstand children, and so on. If the teacher has inadequate understanding of those he or she is attempting to teach in terms of what they bring to the situation, then the process of teaching is reduced to random activity where children learn *despite* what is being attempted. Quite possibly some do 'learn' in this way throughout their school lives, especially brighter children. A child's inability to give direct feedback about what is wrong when he or she fails to 'read' or understand a principle of mathematics puts him or her in the same situation as the car driver. Perhaps this is why John Dewey as long ago as 1916 pessimistically noted that:

> no thought can possibly be conveyed as an idea from one person to another — the communication may stimulate the other person to realise the question for himself and to think out a like idea, or it may smother his intellectual interest and suppress his dawning effort at thought . . . When the parent or teacher has provided the conditions which stimulate thinking and has taken a sympathetic attitude towards the activities of the learner *by entering into a common or conjoint experience,* all has been done which a second party can do to instigate learning. *(Dewey, 1916)*

It is important to note that Dewey emphasises the *social* nature of learning, a point many educators have not so far understood or accepted.

PSYCHOLOGICAL THEORIES

A number of psychological theories have provided useful models of behaviour and insights into many aspects of the development of children: those of Piaget, Vigotsky, Bruner and Freud are perhaps the foremost and best known. But these theories attempt to explain certain facets of behaviour which, while of practical value to the teacher, do not consider the child and his or her settings in an overall way. Other theories in psychology are concerned with 'bits' of a person and of behaviour to an even greater extent. There are theories of intelligence, theories of motivation, theories of 'cognitive dissonance', etc., parallel to a chemist having a theory about the composition of copper without reference to the physical world (Bannister and Fransella, 1980). These bits of the person are usually termed traits and psychologists following these kinds of theories see humans as being made up of them. The underlying idea behind studying the bits we are supposedly composed of is that once we know all about the bits we can predict the best ways for humans to develop and obviate the worst. The argument against a trait theory lies in our use of words: it is not only useful common coinage to talk of demonstrating intelligent, well-motivated, distinctly idiosyncratic etc. behaviour; we do behave (sometimes) in these ways, but it does not follow that we 'have' such static, enduring characteristics. However, the greatest problem with trait 'theory' is twofold: it doesn't predict at all well and it presents a picture of ourselves which does not test well against our experience of ourselves. If I experience myself as being made up of 'bits', I am not necessarily aware of being composed of such kinds of bits as I monitor my behaviour from one minute to another or one situation to another. I may, of course, conceive of myself in this way after having read a psychology textbook, and further, the plausibility of such a theory may lie in the sense of identity I might wish to hold on to by such notions. In the classroom the teacher can reify a child's bits and pieces and in doing so turn him or her into a virtually unchanging event which serves an obvious purpose when the teacher is trying to cope as efficiently and effectively as possible with thirty children: it is a convenience with scientific approval. That the child may not see him or herself in this way is not the point of what might be achieved by ignoring the child's version. But practising as well as academic psychologists may well support the teacher in seeing children as so composed: there are many different kinds of tests they use where such a view — that of hypothetical constructs — is the underlying rationale by which to characterise the child.

The other major psychological theory applied to children in the classroom is that termed 'behaviourism'.[1] In behaviourist psychology the static characteristics of a child's traits fade into an unidentifiable child whose behaviour is functionally related only to the situations he or she is in. This immediately looks like, and is, an oddly unpredicated notion, as we have no idea who has defined the situation. Certainly in a behaviouristic rationale we don't attempt to get the child's version, but usually rely on that of the teacher initially, and when things go wrong,

---

[1] I use the term in the classical Skinnerian sense: a model still claimed as having powerful practical application in the classroom. I am not referring to later 'behavioural' models such as direct instruction and precision teaching.

changes and supplements supplied by psychologists if they are well disposed to the theory.

Much of the claimed success of behaviourism in the classroom, the product of its plausibility, lies in the apparent ability to shape desired behaviour. It must be said at once that this is perfectly possible. This activity is dependent on two things: that it is possible to apply strict control contingencies (though 'control' is never strictly defined by Skinner and I use the word in his loose way: perhaps we can imagine a jail-type institutional situation here) and that the behaviour put in perspective can be seen as trivial (e.g. out-of-seat behaviour), short-lasting, and not generalisable. Follow-up studies to those of the application of behaviouristic principles in the classroom are hard to find.

The position of behaviourism appears to be all or nothing. Self-styled classroom autocrats can claim it for their very own and believe in it, provided they don't follow the child beyond the classroom door.

OTHER THEORETICAL POSITIONS

A serious omission from these two models of behaviour is the person as being the author of his or her own behaviour. If I am made up of bits, it is the bits that 'cause' me to behave in the way I do. If the environment is responsible for my behaviour, then only changing the environment can change my behaviour. I have no say whatsoever either way. In the sense that our behaviour is predictable to an extent, we can be said to 'have traits' (in a vague way), and it is undeniable that certain environmental events appear to cause some of our behaviour.

At a much earlier time than the Dewey quote above, Immanuel Kant made a similar point: 'neither experience nor thought can be understood as things that happen to us, but only as things that we do' (Harre and Secord, 1972), stressing the sense of agency in the person who is learning. The recent theoretical position of 'hermeneutical psychology' (Gauld and Shotter, 1977) conjoins the notion of self-as-agent with that of self-as-interpreter of events.

There are now a number of theories which bear remarkable similarities to each other, all of which emphasise that we are *interpreters of our world:* that there is no such thing as 'environment', but only what we understand it to be, and thus we act according to our understandings.

The foremost proponent of the model man-the-interpreter is George Kelly, whose work, although he died in 1967, has not until recently become generally well known in either academic or practising psychology;

in fact it is still infinitely less 'influential' than the psychologies noted above and quite unknown as applied to education. Yet it can be claimed for personal construct psychology (PCP) (Kelly, 1955), inasmuch as it is about how people make sense of their surroundings, a relevance for educational theory and practice which could help to transform the kinds of rigidity and false approaches which at present limit everyone involved in educational ventures. There are a number of reasons for the slow development of PCP: it is in some central respects unnerving (self as construct — see below); although easy to grasp in its main ideas, it has a depth and complexity which match the way we experience ourselves; to describe it, Kelly was forced to invent quite a large vocabulary of new terms, and the way he expresses his ideas is sometimes difficult to grasp at first reading; also the theory in many ways looks like common sense (in a number of ways it is) and perhaps because of this its radical shift from other kinds of psychology is not immediately apparent. Thus Kelly's ideas in general have been misunderstood, labelled unoriginal, or ignored.

Kelly's basic idea is that 'all men' (even babies) 'are scientists', by which he means that the way in which we come to understand ourselves, our surroundings and other people is by creating hypotheses about what kinds of events we seem to be experiencing. In attempting to make sense of our interactions, with others, we 'design experiments' in order to test out these hypotheses, and our 'conclusions' about what is a reasonable interpretation rest on our 'experimental results': whether they validate or invalidate our hypotheses. In other words, what characterises human behaviour fundamentally is that we are inquirers about events and our behaviour rests on our interpretation of them. We are also, reflexively, a focus of our inquiry. Kelly devised strategies (grid techniques) which, instead of employing the usual psychologist's device of telling people what kind of event the psychologist has found them to be (an introvert, neurotic, etc.), consist of *asking the person* in such a way that the answers (constructs) can be structured in order to reflect the ways in which that person can see his or her own strategies at work when attempting to make sense of his or her surroundings. All behaviour', maintains Kelly, 'is an experiment'. Thus the teacher can never be sure that what he or she does will have the desired effect. Selves are self-constructed: other people don't make us what we are, but we ourselves are the authors of ourselves in the way we interpret both our ongoing behaviour and the ways in which others see us. Teachers and children are, therefore (as are all people; this, according to Kelly, is the main feature of our behaviour in relating to others), both 'experiments' and are constantly and predominantly in the process of experimenting with each other. We are simultaneously carrying out experiments on ourselves as we are experimenting with our version of others. Different versions of events come to mind, but some will be more compelling than others because, *for our purposes*, they predict with greater accuracy.

The third and last important idea relevant here is Kelly's notion of 'transcending the obvious'. He maintains that the conclusions we come to often rest in various forms of required consensus (the conversational 'you know what I mean', 'surely you would agree'). We couldn't co-operate without such devices. But, notes Kelly, *nothing* is truly 'obvious': in going beyond the apparent nature of things, in carefully listening and further inquiring, nothing remains entirely as it has been seen to be. Children 'live up to the expectations' of teacher and parent (and education authority) only to the extent that people wish to see them doing that. Holding on to the obvious is another expedient which helps us to cope with life in some ways, but can lead to denying the fact that people (and children more quickly) change not according to their circumstances (for objectively these do not exist) but as they themselves interpret their circumstances. People, and especially children at times, often do not wish to follow the expectations of others.

Kelly is not alone in this kind of model. Sociologists such as Mead (Strauss, 1964) and Berger and Luckman (1971) and the ethnomethodologists (Garfinkel, 1967) Gauld and Shotter (1977) are like-minded, but not as elaborately detailed in their descriptions of the 'mechanics' of behaviour as Kelly.

The last model I would briefly like to draw attention to, which has an equally powerful relevance to the educational futures of children, comes from research in child development, particularly that where the behaviour of very young babies has been under scrutiny. This now clearly demonstrates (e.g. Bower, 1979; Condon and Sander, 1974; Schaffer, 1971) that the newly born child behaves in relation to caretakers in a social way which is as much initiatory as receptive. This demonstration has come about largely through the use of stopped video frames which show movement that cannot be seen by the naked eye. It can be seen, for instance, that almost from the moment of birth babies can 'slot in' at very rapid speeds to the movements and gestures of the caretaker, and initiate behaviour which appears to contain the intention of expecting appropriately 'slotted-in' responses. Within the first year the development of this innately programmed skill has developed into clearly intentioned and highly sophisticated social behaviour (e.g. peek-a-boo) which features as a prime component the kinds of experimental search for prediction through validation/invalidation theoretically postulated by Kelly. (Kelly said he saw the baby's world as 'sliced by co-ordinates' of *x*s and *y*s going together or the opposite in the baby's developing sense of agency and experimentation.)

CONCLUSION

I end by suggesting that we can make sense of children learning only if we take the position that in many senses the child begins life essentially as, and continues to be, a learning process: it is not something he or she has or has not. It is not a trait. Neither is the child 'determined' by his or her external circumstances, unless these are of a jail-type coerciveness, for 'environment' is an extremely complex series of events, both limiting and enhancing in so many ways. It is only in the nature of the interaction between children and their world, in the sense children make of the environment, that they develop, elaborate their self and their understanding of what exists outside them. But a restricted, official view of learning operates to develop less than a quarter of the child population by an examination system which labels the remainder as failures, and psychology has done much to underwrite the validity of such a view. For instance, it has attempted to devise ways in which to 'motivate' children in an information force-feeding process which implies an otherwise ill-nourished or starved mind. It trains educational psychologists to test 'intelligence' and even 'personality' in order to discover how able the child is for this undertaking. It seems no exaggeration to say that in ensuring a sense of educational failure in three-quarters of our child population we commit a tragic and apparently cold-blooded act. It is not difficult to find evidence that no child enjoys being seen as a failure or having had only partial success in such a system, and a psychology which serves it unwittingly or otherwise is as censurable as the system itself.

'System', however, is a vague word, and villains vanish as we try to track them down. It is easy to blame teacher, head teacher and home background. When we observe teaching it is often difficult to imagine what sense the child can make of what the teacher is attempting, and teachers may rightly question the validity of what they are asked to do by a head teacher and an education authority which has to decide what constitutes a 'useful' curriculum. In many respects the curriculum is an arbitrary event dependent on many factors, not least on the demands of university-imposed examination systems, on historic traditions, and on our ignorance of what may best enhance a child's development on this still magnificently endowed planet. The newer psychologies ask that we focus, in the child's development, on his or her sense of agency (Shotter, 1975) and on the notion that centrally the child is an interpreter of the world. In particular, and in specifying the implications of these ideas, it seems to me that curriculum and teaching strategies should pivot around four central conditions of childhood:

1. Children are born innately programmed to act and respond in *a social way to a social world.* They must constantly test out their own versions of themselves alongside those of others in order to increase their understanding of human events. Donne's sixteenth-century perception that 'no man is an island' is illustrated every day in psychopathology, in social psychology and above all in our everyday lives; learning cannot take place in a vacuum, though classroom silence implies that silence is sine qua non to the process of learning.

2. Inasmuch as the child *is* a learning process, he or she is *a scientific kind of event,* that is, the strategies by which he or she comes to an understanding of the world, both physical and human, are those of scientific inquiry. Children are born scientists in that to increase their understanding they must work out what goes with what (Kelly's world as 'sliced by co-ordinates'). The kinaesthetic feedback they receive from their fingers touching an object which then begins to move is related to the visible movement of fingers and object. When their parents shout they associate this with disapproval or imminent danger. They also extract from the data of their existence what seems to be of most or more peripheral importance, and accordingly group the data. Without factor analysis, analysing variation and correlating, the baby, child or adult could make no sense of events. Perhaps the largest irony of teaching is that we teach, often badly, mathematics and science to a very skilled mathematician-scientist, an observation rich in its implications for the future.

3. The child is *born into a moral world,* to which extent he or she must be a moral event. Children are forever illustrating this in their remarks about what is fair and what is not fair. The beginnings of delinquency, criminality and everyday classroom cussedness are born in this fact of existence. One of the most vivid expressions of it comes not from psychology, though Piaget (1932) describes moral processes well, but from the novelist Joyce Cary in *Charley is my Darling.* In the preface to the 1951 edition (four years before the publication of Kelly's *Psychology of Personal Constructs*) he wrote:

    > . . . The world that stands to be explored (by children) is a moral structure which, simply because it is one of related ideas, is much harder for (the child) to grasp. He perceives that it is there, he feels

its importance to his comfort and security every moment of the day, but it is not present to his eyes and ears: he cannot see and touch it. He is not equipped with the experience and judgement necessary to put it together for himself. For this purpose nature has provided him . . . with parents. And if they refuse the duty of making a situation clear to him he will suffer . . . Without such a picture, children don't know where they are, and they do all kinds of evil (because it is just this sphere of good and evil that is puzzling them) to find out. A child will torture a cat or some other smaller child in order to see what will happen, both to himself and the victim, and what he feels like in the new circumstances. The 'crime' is a moral experiment *(Cary, 1951)*.

When schools 'invalidate' children by failing them, confusing and confounding them with curricula apparently unrelated to their existence, they present them with a central moral issue that the children have to face with mechanical acceptance, withdrawal or hatred. As other writers in this book show, there can be no issue of greater importance to education.

4. Last, we can go beyond Kelly in claiming that *'man (and the child) is a psychologist'*. We are forced into this (but are, as is psychology, partly equipped to cope with problems as they appear) by our existence in the car driver's position, having to read ambiguous signals and noises and attempting to make sense of them, in order to make the best of the journey and finish it safely. To do this we must predict the intentions of others and make corresponding sense of our own intentions and behaviour. In reflecting on (interpreting, researching) what we and others do in the situations we find ourselves in, we adjust our behaviour according to the anticipations and interpretations we have made.

To relate these four notions, we can say that the education of children must work from a position which increases its understanding of children as essentially social beings who elaborate themselves within a moral context by means of their strategies of scientific and psychological inquiry (and one can argue quite clearly that their artistic and emotional selves are intimately related to these in developing their version of the world; it is easy to slip back into a trait model). These should be the starting points of education, for they can be seen as being, I would argue, the principal features of children's everyday behaviour, an assertion which can be tested out by the reader by keeping a diary of a child's behaviour over a day or two. The child is truly the father of the man, the author and agent of his or her present and future behaviour. The adult, of course, may not choose to see children in this way. It would appear to follow, therefore, that education in its present structures and curricula is misjudged, because the nature of children and the way they come to understand their existence have so far been misinterpreted. We *can* graft on knowledge in a coercive system, but such knowledge is worthless when it does not follow children's own channels of inquiry. We cannot 'motivate' them because, as Kelly pointed out, they are already 'motivated' in being active inquirers into increasing their understanding. That is not only their birthright, it is the nature and condition of their existence.

It should follow from this that the training of educators — teachers, head teachers, administrators, parents — must have as its first concern that nature and condition. It also follows that psychology should be able to advise on and aid the implementation of a fresh start. This could be done initially only in experimental terms: the setting up of schools where new types of curricula and teaching methods could be attempted, and where evaluation is built in from the inception and focuses on how the children respond in their own words rather than producing data from observation and academic results, in the way the majority of research is conducted.

However, before such experiments are carried out, it seems logical to argue for yet another, but far more comprehensive, reconsidering of what education should centrally involve. Listening to what people say about their schooling and remembering what happened in our own, it would be difficult to conclude that it was this which now enables us to cope with the complexities of our world, the complexity which is our self, and that which is other people. When we scrutinise curricula it is not easy to imagine how today's children will look back at their schooldays as a time that improved their ability to widen their channels of inquiry as a lifelong process. Nor is it evident how psychologies which reduce people to caricatures of puppets or view them as a single-solution jigsaw puzzle are going to clarify the difficulties involved in this task. To argue that while education systems, curricula and teaching styles remain as they are, the psychologies we subscribe to and practise should also remain is in my opinion a radical error, for it is the psychologies which emphasise notions of control and static models of children which have helped to create the educational systems we have.

To me it follows that a conjunction of psychology and education in the future must focus on children as psychologists, and foremost on the sense we make of them not as 'learners' but as people. Neither psychology nor education can yet comprehensively detail ways of doing this, but both are at the crossroads of making crucial decisions about their futures and joint paths, at a time when humankind cannot afford another large error of judgement.

REFERENCES

Bannister, D. and Fransella, F. (1980) *Inquiring Man.* Harmondsworth: Penguin.

Berger, P. and Luckman, T. (1971) *The Social Construction of Reality.* Harmondsworth: Penguin.

Bower, T.G.R. (1979) *Human Development.* San Francisco: W.H. Freeman.

Cary, J. (1951) *Charley Is My Darling.* London: Michael Joseph (Carfax Edition).

Condon, W.S. and Sander, L. (1974) Neonate movement is synchronized with adult speech, *Science,* **183**, pp. 99–101.

Cox, C.B. and Dyson, A.E. (ed.) (1969, 1972) *Black Paper One; Black Paper Two.* London: The Critical Quarterly Society.

Dewey, J. (1916) *Democracy and Education.* London: Macmillan.

Dockar Drysdale, B. (1968) *Therapy in Child Care.* Harlow: Longman.

Garfinkel, H. (1967) *Studies in Ethnomethodology.* Hemel Hempstead: Prentice-Hall.

Gauld, A. and Shotter, J. (1977) *Human Action and its Psychological Investigation.* London: Routledge & Kegan Paul.

Harre, R. and Secord, P.F. (1972) *The Explanation of Social Behaviour.* Oxford: Basil Blackwell.

Kelly, G.A. (1955) *The Psychology of Personal Constructs.* New York: Norton.

Piaget, J. (1932) *The Moral Judgement of the Child.* London: Routledge & Kegan Paul.

Schaffer, H.R. (1971) *The Growth of Sociability.* Harmondsworth: Penguin.

Shotter, J. (1975) *Images of Man in Psychological Research.* London: Methuen.

Strauss, A. (ed.) (1964) *George Herbert Mead on Social Psychology.* London: University of Chicago Press.

8
State-supported alternative schools

Laura Diamond
(on behalf of CSSAS)

THE NEED FOR ALTERNATIVE SCHOOLS

Every person is both unique and one out of many millions of people, all-important and utterly insignificant. If from birth we seem to matter to others, if we feel well looked after and loved in an undemanding way, we can grow up seeing ourselves as valuable and accept our insignificance in the universe without too much anxiety. Such love frees us to use our energies and ingenuity for many purposes other than to attract attention and to prove our importance to ourselves and others. It allows us to explore, experiment and learn for the sheer interest of it and therefore it also helps us to find, as we become more knowledgeable, competent and creative, new forms of nurture which continue to sustain us throughout life.

In other words, learning is intimately linked with love and contentment in a well-known cycle. This is commonly accepted and would hardly need stating if, in the context of schooling, it were not all too often narrowed down to mean that children who are loved and happy at home are likely to learn well at school and that children who do not do well at school are likely to come from unloving or otherwise inadequate homes. Neither follows automatically. How successful a school is at helping children to learn depends very largely on whether the school itself is nurturing besides being competent. Obviously no child — whether loved or unloved at home — finds much of interest to do and learn at a dull school with unresourceful teachers, and even children from very happy homes are likely to learn much less than they could and with much less pleasure in an emotionally arid, uncongenial environment where they feel that no-one except a friend or two cares much

91

about them personally. Children today, in the UK as in most societies, spend many hours at school with adults other than their parents and therefore the attitude of these adults will have an important effect on how the children see themselves. Unless any sense of worth they have gained at home is confirmed and reinforced by the school, their emotional needs will not be fully met and this will affect both their personality and their learning. It goes without saying that children who feel unloved at home need support at school all the more.

Unfortunately, few schools have ever truly accepted that acting *in loco parentis* means, perhaps above all, being loving, making each child feel valued and important, as parents are rightly expected to do. The neglect by the schools of their nurturing role, detrimental at all times, is bound to affect all the more the young of today, for whom building up self-esteem and self-confidence in a world which feels bigger and more hostile is more difficult. To earlier generations the size of the world and the world population were only abstract facts. Transport was slower, television did not exist and the world felt smaller and less crushing because people saw less of it and did not hear what went on everywhere all the time. Children moved in narrower, less impersonal circles where at least they were known. There was also more free space, even in the cities, where they could play or meet their friends without transgressing some adult rule or some adult's right. They felt less anonymous and less ill-at-ease outside the home. Today's children are faced from a much younger age with the reality of their personal insignificance in the world. They also learn sooner that most adults do not carry much weight either, and this usually includes their own parents, which cannot be very reassuring. While, in a way, this cutting down to size of the adults puts them closer to the children and makes them easier to understand and get on with, adulthood now looks less glossy to those approaching it; it has less to do with power and prestige and more to do with hard work and responsibilities. Though adolescents still see it as a more desirable status than a childhood without rights, they are bound to feel more apprehensive about making a life of their own in a complex, formidable society dominated by vast, powerful structures which seem to overawe and confuse even the adults.

In brief, in our present world a sense of security is harder to maintain for everyone, and particularly for the young. It is therefore more important than ever that adults caring for children should do their best to help them build up their self-esteem and self-confidence. Fortunately, from this point of view, the family has evolved in the right direction. For all its disadvantages, the nuclear family has led to greater contact and more intense feelings between its members and hence to a greater sense of personal identity for all. More closely observed by their more knowing children, parents now find it more difficult to play God and lay down the law, and most interact with their children on a more equal footing. Therefore, while feeling more suppressed and insignificant outside the home, children today are generally more able to assert themselves within the home and gain there a good deal of confidence. Schools, on the other hand, have evolved considerably less. At a time when adults themselves seek greater informality and comradeship with one another, possibly to fight increased feelings of insignificance, at most schools adults and children continue to interact formally and on an unequal basis, with the children firmly kept at the bottom of a hierarchy. Though discipline is less harsh, the emphasis is still on children learning what they are told, doing as they are told, forgetting their own likes and dislikes and generally suppressing their feelings at school as if, in the context of education, feelings and inclinations were not only an irrelevance but also an obstacle. Little affection flows, and little real respect is established. The children's views are suppressed, few opportunities are given to them for making choices and taking responsibility, initiative is little encouraged. Only those children who perform well at set tasks gain much notice and appreciation, so the less intelligent and the less compliant receive little nurture from the school.

Of course this general approach clashes with that of the modern family, where not only the emotional climate but also the style of teaching is different. Parents now tend to preach less and to teach more by their example. Their behaviour is questioned and they try to justify their demands. They allow argument and can admit their mistakes. Generally less impressed by adults and used to more dialogue and negotiation in the family, today's children do not think much of the insistence of many of their teachers on unquestioning conformity. Though most do comply, for they have no option, their respect for the school is not very great.

Because of this, many schools say that parents undermine their authority. This is true. By their own teaching style and by their more democratic interactions with their children, parents inevitably undermine the authority of schools which insist, as still so many do, on automatic obedience. At the same time, paradoxically, very many parents support or at least condone the schools' authoritarian ways and wish to see little change made. The reasons behind this puzzling fact are numerous: many parents are confused and intimidated by the schools' self-righteousness and their refusal to reassess their own methods; many just cannot imagine school being any different from what they knew themselves; perhaps above all, many parents believe that by the well-tried means of selection, competition and compulsion schools are more likely than by other methods to maximise their own children's chances of getting on in the world. Though more democratic, the family is now more insular. Less supported by others, many parents feel very heavily the responsibilities of parenthood and in return they accept little obligation except towards their own children. They work very hard for a better standard of living for themselves and their children and expect their children to do likewise when they grow up. Such parents, who are possibly the vast majority, see the main role of the school as equipping their children with the paper qualifications and the competing attitude required for economic and social success in the world today. However, because they love their children and wish them to be happy now as well as in the future, they also want to believe that their children enjoy school quite a lot, despite their apparent lack of enthusiasm, as if children could enjoy school while being forced, with their parents' consent, to learn things that bore them by teachers whose authoritarian manner their parents have in practice taught them to resent and despise. In consequence, many parents prefer not to look too closely at what goes on at their children's school. This is unfortunate, for in many instances what goes on is that their children, deprived of all autonomy and pushed back into the crowd, are losing at school much of the self-confidence they have built up at home and are neither learning much nor having a very happy time. Sadly, many parents discover their children's failure too late and with great pain, and they do not even then understand the real reasons for it. Some blame lack of discipline, some shortage of funds, and some black parents blame racialism. By attributing the lack of success of so many pupils to shortage of funds or racialism, which are indeed additional factors, its main causes become obscured. These must be found in the ethos and practice of the schools.

Innumerable demands are put on the schools: the children need love, stimulation and guidance; parents want paper qualifications based on a rigid and inequitable examination system; the politicians of the left insist on discrimination in favour of the more disadvantaged children; the politicians of the right insist on discrimination in favour of the brightest; the public want to see good examination results as hard proof of success. Under so many conflicting pressures, the schools can hardly do well by everybody. Those which do not try, and which opt openly for satisfying some of these demands, as many private schools do, stand a chance of fulfilling their aims and can be seen to succeed. Many state schools, though, which are under the greatest pressures, try to respond to all while pretending to be following only their own professional judgement, and end up satisfying no-one fully, least of all the children. Disturbed by this, many of their most sensitive and therefore potentially best teachers drop out of teaching.

Do schools, though failing to meet the children's needs, at least fulfil the needs of society? Hardly, when, because of tradition and parental pressure, they persist in stimulating competition among their pupils as preparation for life in an overpopulated world where technological progress has been used in such a way that enormous power can now be achieved by a few, while millions of people have very little chance of ever raising themselves above subsistence level through individual effort alone. By encouraging children to work hard mainly for personal success while offering them few opportunities for joint work with others, and criticising them for interesting themselves in their friends in the classroom, the schools serve the needs of society no more than those of the individual children. They could have claimed to serve the former when the progress of humankind seemed to depend on the intensive exploitation of the earth's resources. However, its progress and perhaps its survival now seem much more dependent on the potential winners of the power game declining to seek gratification through power and choosing, out of feeling for their fellow beings, to share with them on a fair basis whatever is left of the earth's resources. Helping the young to grow up with feeling for one another and to develop the wish and the capacity to co-operate with others for common success is the contribution towards the improvement of society which schools should now aim for. In fact, by continuing to emphasise competition much more than co-operation schools are not even preparing the young adequately for employment today, for the ability to work as part of a team is now required in so many jobs that most employers consider it a basic skill.

Other faults of the schools — the obsolescence of the curriculum, the emphasis on intellectual skills to the detriment of others, the inability to teach anything at all to some children — are easier to remedy, at least superficially, and efforts to do so are already being made by some schools. Meeting children's increased nurturing needs, developing their sensitivity to others and preparing them better for an autonomous and responsible life in a rather frightening and endangered world require a transformation of the schools which at present neither the schools themselves nor, unfortunately, most parents seem able to envisage. Until parents in particular come to realise the benefits that children derive from truly caring and democratic schools and put their weight behind widespread reform in this direction, such a reform will be virtually impossible to achieve. Even if one of the political parties when in power wanted to introduce this reform from above — and none of the parties is showing such an intention at the moment — its implementation would be most arduous and ineffectual if parents could be said to be against it. If parents are to be persuaded, theoretical argument will not be enough. They must be able to see the benefits of such schools with their own eyes, which means that more need to be formed. Those parents, teachers and others who do see the urgent need for a radical change in the ways in which adults interact with children in schools must get together to promote alternative schools such as those about to be described and must be prepared to work for their success at least until they are well established, with some financial security and in the hands of people equally committed to their philosophy. The pioneering work of these alternative schools should, in time, make an impact and encourage widespread reform.

THE SCHOOLS

In what way would alternative schools differ from others? What would their basic features be? The Campaign for State-Supported Alternative Schools proposes a model which is, it feels, uniquely suited to the achievement of uncontroversial objectives which are professed by the majority of educationists and pursued in theory by most schools: to help children to develop their potential fully and grow up into self-confident and responsible adults. As shown in the previous section, CSSAS believes that schools are failing in their objectives largely because of their undemocratic and hierarchical structure; the distance they create between adults and children impedes the development of pupils' self-confidence and of the capacity to feel and handle responsibility. CSSAS proposes a model of alternative schools which simply seeks to put theory into practice and in fact does no more than bring into the school the democratic principles on which our society is ostensibly based and which have begun to take root in the family.

Such a school would be democratic, open, non-hierarchical, non-coercive, non-violent and small.

Democratic

On the basis of equality, school students, parents and workers would be involved fully in the making of decisions affecting them, primarily at regular meetings with open agenda. This would be in contrast to conventional schools which tend to exclude parents, school students, assistant teachers and other staff from the decision-making processes. The mechanisms by which democratic schools can run have been pioneered on a national scale in countries like Finland and Denmark, and in particular schools (e.g. Countesthorpe and White Lion Street) in this country.

In such a school, democracy and co-operation could be learned from an early age in the most effective way possible, through practice. The problems which our world faces are likely to have reached alarming proportions by the time today's children have grown up. Only confident, discerning adults, used to facing problems as a matter of course and to taking part in their solution on an equal basis with others, will have a chance of tackling these major issues successfully.

Open

The alternative school would be open in five ways:

1. It would be open to anyone who wanted to go there. Selection or discrimination of any sort would not be practised. It would not, however, be open to children whose parents did not wish them to go there, or to school students who did not want to go there themselves. In the event of the school being oversubscribed, procedures would be worked out in consultation with the local education authority (though the demand might be taken as evidence of the need for another alternative school).

2. It would be open in the way that a few schools already are: parents and others wishing to come in and help would be welcomed. The benefit of this would be more than the tapping of extra skills and goodwill, valuable as this is. It would facilitate contact between children and friendly adults in their neighbourhood who are prepared to interest themselves in children other than their own. This might be a step towards the opening up of the nuclear family, which by its insularity makes parenthood burdensome and puts many children at risk.

3. It would be open as much of the time as possible. In so far as staffing allowed, it could be open during the evenings, weekends and holidays: the human capacity to learn is not active only between 9 o'clock and 4 o'clock on 200 days a year.

4. As far as resources allowed, it would be open to all who wanted to learn, whatever their age and qualifications. Education need not be confined to those between the ages of five and nineteen.

5. It would be open in the sense of making its aims and structures explicit. Its meetings, proceedings, minutes, reports and records would be open to those concerned.

Non-hierarchical

It is not only that this is a more comfortable and productive way for adults to work together, it is part of the CSSAS democratic perspective that children should be able to learn — by *example* as well as by instruction — that co-operation and consensus are the best ways of proceeding.

For the same reason, children should be able to see that the ordinary routines of life — cleaning, cooking, repairing, administering — do not demean our existence but enrich it. Thus workers at the school would avoid as far as possible the division of labour which in our society has gone well beyond the bounds of necessity.

Therefore a job-sharing system would be encouraged. This has the added advantage of improving the adult:student ratio at no extra cost. For example, in an Inner London junior school with 200 students, there are 11.5 teachers — a student:teacher ratio of 17.3:1. There are, in addition, nine ancillary workers (non-teaching staff like cooks, cleaners and clerical workers), giving a ratio of students to school-workers of 9.7:1. It is worth noting that, according to ILEA's Annual Abstract for 1976, the ratio of students to staff, including non-teaching staff, in the Inner London area is 4.5:1.

Non-coercive

CSSAS is convinced that children learn more effectively and develop a far deeper commitment to learning when they can make their own choices than when choices are made for them. One can force children into specific rooms for specific periods, but one cannot enforce successful learning. Therefore, while the alternative school would have to abide by the law on compulsory attendance, there would be no compulsory lessons or any compulsory curriculum. Initiative, self-direction, self-discipline and negotiation would be the watchwords. Adults would advise and help the children, but they would neither coerce them nor manipulate them into taking part in particular activities. Whether they could or should encourage them to take on activities which they, the adults, consider valuable seems best left to each individual school to decide at its democratic general meetings. The same applies to the choice of internal forms of assessment. Older students, of course, would be helped to prepare themselves for any public examinations they might decide to sit.

Non-violent

Punishment in general is wretched, inefficient and inappropriate for a learning community. Physical punishment of any kind is completely unacceptable under any circumstances.

Small

In order to ensure that the democratic procedures of the alternative school function with the full involvement of all students and adult workers and that each individual is known as a person rather than as a face or a name, it is felt that the school community (or the autonomous units of which it is made up if some form of federal model is chosen) should not comprise more than 200 people.

Schools of this size are already considered desirable at the junior-school level. However, to provide the expensive facilities required by older students it would be necessary to establish a system of co-ordinated units. These units, each with a high degree of autonomy, could share either purpose-built facilities on a campus basis — as has been done in certain areas of the USA, such as Minneapolis, in Australia, at Morialta High, Adelaide, and in New Zealand with the 'whanau' family structure — or existing public amenities — libraries, sports facilities, spare space in labs in further education colleges, etc. This latter arrangement, more appropriate in urban areas, has been successful in cities as far apart as New York ('City-as-School') and Christchurch, New Zealand (Four Avenues School).

PUBLIC FUNDING

Experience has shown that lack of funds is one of the major problems met by groups which want to set up or which have set up an alternative school. The schools proposed by CSSAS would be open to all and it follows that they could not, and would not want to, charge fees. Therefore, for them to enjoy a necessary degree of security and be free from constant financial preoccupations which would hinder their work, they would require public funding. CSSAS believes that they are entitled to it.

In several countries — Denmark in particular — groups of parents, school students and teachers can set up their own schools, according to their own values and priorities, with most or all of the capital and running costs coming from public funds. In this country alternative choices already exist within the maintained sector: church schools, single-sex schools and schools which emphasise the academic tradition of the grammar schools. However, maintained education has a much poorer record when it comes to meeting the demands for innovatory alternatives. The existing choices are, in fact, even further removed than most ordinary state schools from the open, democratic structure which CSSAS believes to be essential for the satisfactory personal and social development of children today. There is at present within the state system no alternative choice available to those who find the mainstream schools too authoritarian and outdated.

This is not to say that only the type of alternative school proposed by CSSAS has a justifiable claim on state funding. No doubt a good case could be made for other types, and CSSAS believes that all claims should be considered. In a democratic society, choice should be everyone's right rather than the privilege of those who can afford to pay, and such a right should become embedded in the law.

There is no doubt that at present demands vary greatly among parents and professionals because they see differently the failings of schools. Indeed, intense debate continues over such questions as: 'traditional' versus 'progressive' teaching methods; the monopoly over curriculum exercised by the teaching profession; the amount of streaming and setting that should take place in schools; the optimum size of schools; the importance of having schools that have close links with the community; the relative influence of teachers, parents, school students, educational policy-makers and the community as a whole in the governing bodies of schools; and many more. Yet, when the time comes for an issue to be resolved, the diversity of views is usually ignored and decisions are made by the Department of Education and Science for the country as a whole, by a local education authority for a county or borough, or by head teachers for their schools.

Often the result is that the views of those who claim to represent the majority are forced upon frustrated minorities. Thus parents who strongly disapprove of streaming may be forced to send their children to a local school where the practice has strong support among the teaching staff; others who favour small community schools may have to put up with seeing their children bussed to a remote, 1500-student institution; and parents who take an active interest in their children's education and in the affairs of the school may be faced with a head teacher who regards them as busybodies threatening to undermine his or her authority and that of the professional staff. Finally, there are parents, school students and indeed many teachers whose educational priorities are not being met at all within the structure of existing schools.

All these situations, which cause needless disappointment to significant groups of people, arise from our tendency to settle discussions on public policy issues by the simple expedient of imposing the will of the majority on everyone else. There are, indeed, areas where this is necessary: the state can have only one policy on nuclear deterrence and the same traffic regulations must be obeyed by all. In many fields, however, including that of educational policy, a diversity of solutions and practices could coexist and individuals and groups could pursue different objectives without either infringing each other's rights or harming the general interest. To impose the same policies on everybody is a sure way of making the work of the schools extremely difficult and dooming them to failure.

CSSAS believes that choice within the state system guaranteed by the force of law would strengthen rather than weaken the state system for two reasons: it would stop the disaffection of many parents who look for a solution to their anxieties outside the system and it would protect it from the damages caused by the erratic changes of party political control.

It is essential, however, that the law should include limitations on the exercise of the right to promote particular types of schools, as there are with respect to all democratic choices. The exercise of one's freedom must not have harmful effects on other people (including, of course, one's own children) or on the community as a whole. This applies all the more when one is seeking to use public money.

Certain conditions should be satisfied by all alternative schemes before they are granted local authority support. Most of these are based on the implicit or explicit criteria applied to all existing maintained schools. Others have been added to prevent schemes from promoting the interests of some groups of citizens to the detriment of others and to safeguard children from the misguided zeal of cranks or over-anxious parents:

1. They should be non-fee-paying.
2. They should be non-selective on grounds of ability or aptitude.
3. They should not discriminate in their admission policy nor in their activities on grounds of race, colour, nationality, sex or religion.
4. They should have to state in extensive detail their goals and their proposed structure and methods, and argue the particular benefits of the scheme from the point of view of those most directly concerned, i.e. the children.

5. They should show that there is sufficient demand in the LEA area to justify the proposed scheme.
6. They should accept inspection by Her Majesty's Inspectors in order to be assessed as educationally efficient, though HMIs would be expected to respect the stated aims and values of the school in making their assessment; they should accept inspection by local fire and health inspectors.
7. The governing body should include representatives from the community, the world of education and the maintaining authority.

IMPLEMENTATION

The alternative schools proposed by CSSAS would conform fully to these conditions and should, on this basis, qualify for public funding. But how would these schools function in practice? What problems would they meet in attempting to operate so differently from other schools, yet within the constraints of the state system? These are questions which CSSAS has asked itself and has been able to answer with a degree of confidence due to the fact that these proposals are not just untried theories.

A few such schools have existed and still exist and their success in educational terms gives strength to the ideology which has inspired them and on which CSSAS has drawn. By granting funding in September 1982 to the White Lion Street Free School, the Inner London Education Authority was the first local authority to acknowledge the success and the important pioneering role of these schools. CSSAS considers the ILEA's courageous decision a major step forward in the history of the state education system.

In considering public funding for alternative schools, two main areas require attention: those of financial organisation and public accountability.

Finance

Financial arrangements should be made to allow alternative schools more control over their finances than is allowed to maintained schools under the present centrally administered system. The strategy should be merely to re-deploy funds currently being spent by LEAs from one type of school to another. The cost per student of the alternative school should not be greater than that of other maintained schools in an LEA area. Funding would be provided in the form of an annual cash grant. This grant would cover running costs and would be spent as the school decided and in accordance with its principles (e.g. the job-sharing system described above).

Governing body

LEAs would rightly demand the establishment of a satisfactory monitoring system before laying out public money. The normal system of governing bodies, however, is inappropriate to an alternative school, which would require an alternative governing body. In setting up such a body, a local authority should aim to assemble a group of governors who would be experienced and sympathetic to the venture, and able to promote its interests within the customary articles of government.

Attention should be given to the following points:

1. The need for a set of objectives and aims in style and method to be drawn up.
2. An instrument of government, or a contract of responsibilities, to be given by the maintaining authority, which establishes a membership made up of parents, teachers and students (i.e. the users of the school), with other representation from the local community, the world of education, and the maintaining authority itself.
3. The body should be accountable not only to the maintaining authority but to all the others represented, and to the public. Its business should normally be conducted in public; business should be conducted in camera in exceptional circumstances only.
4. The main purpose of the body should be to support the school in the achievement of its aims and objectives.
5. It follows that the body should have responsibility for approving or making appointments of staff.
6. Members of the body should be expected to take a close interest in the school and visit it regularly, preferably to make themselves useful.
7. Members should respect the convention of not interfering in day-to-day detail, which should be left to staff and students.
8. The body should stand between the school and any intrusive media, issuing its own reports from time to time.
9. The body should be prepared to settle disputes whenever possible, and be clear about how its articles provide for reference of such disputes when there is deadlock.

10. Above all, the body should insist upon the maintaining authority fulfilling its obligations to their school.

Although clarity in aims and articles is highly desirable, this does not quite ensure that the new kind of body functions with a style appropriate to the alternative school. In order that it be an 'open' body, and in order wholly to remove the traditional atmosphere of magisterial authority, the following rules might be established:

1. Any member of the school has the right to place an item on an agenda and speak on it.
2. The governing body's decisions must be minuted and published.
3. Whatever powers the governing body has, its attitude should be advisory and supportive and it should aim to resolve conflicts and reach consensus rather than to coerce.
4. In keeping with this, some, if not all, of its meetings should be sociable, for instance concluding with eating, music, dance or games. The governing body would thus celebrate its school's purpose.

9
The deschooling alternative

Dick Kitto

INTRODUCTION

Ten years ago the alternative education boom was at its height: important books (Goodman, 1956, 1971; Holt, 1969, 1970, 1977; Dennison, 1972; Illich, 1971, 1974; Reimer, 1971; Stallibrass, 1977; Postman and Weingartner, 1971; Friere, 1972; Lister, 1974; Motherson, undated) discussing its theoretical basis spilled into the bookshops, the free school movement gained momentum and free schools sprouted like toadstools overnight. The ILEA set up a number of truancy centres whose approach in some cases resembled that of free schools, and these were copied elsewhere. In 1973–74 the raising of the school leaving age inaugurated a rash of ROSLA schemes, some of which were also motivated by the free school approach, though necessarily a watered-down version which went some way towards meeting normal school expectations. A.S. Neill died and the A.S. Neill Trust was set up, mainly by members of the teaching profession, in the hope that it would act as a torch and a catalyst for radical ideas in education. Ivan Illich swept across the English scene like an intellectual tornado, tearing up accepted shibboleths by the roots and proclaiming the deschooled society.

Yet now, only ten years later, the ferment has died. The free school movement didn't get off the ground and is now effectively dead, and ROSLA schemes have begotten no progeny. Illich and the deschoolers are silent, and no voice has replaced them. The heady ideas of an education liberated from the classroom, from the competitive rat race of the examination system, and from the heavy hand of adult expectations and adult conformity, and based instead on children's natural curiosity and natural creativity, seems to have been a chimera. In 1972, Royston Lambert wrote:

> These institutional processes of learning (in schools) . . . are the uniform structure which lurks behind all the varied brands of educational philosophy. They have scarcely ever been questioned. Changes and reform occur within the concept of the school. There has been little attempt in theory and no effort in practice to explore alternative ways for the development of children. *(Lambert, 1972)*

Apart from a few abortive schemes in the 1970s and the growing membership and influence of 'Education Otherwise', and in spite of the powerful voice of Illich, that remains substantially true today. Only the calm, measured voice of John Holt, who in the 1970s still pinned his faith on reform within schools (Holt, 1969, 1970, 1977), now proclaims in unequivocal tones the virtues of deschooling (Holt, 1981).

To be sure, there is quite a lot of experiment and initiative being poured into education, of which the 'Education for Capability' recognition scheme provides evidence. Many of these initiatives are worthy enough, but almost all work within the well-established constraints of the school system: they do not challenge the basic assumptions of compulsory schooling taking place within an institutional framework. Many of them aim to foster creativity, but within closely limited boundaries: technological creativity, entrepreneurial creativity and so on, but always *directed* creativity, directed and controlled and institutionalised to ensure that the scheme fits within the boundaries of the educational system, and that in due course children will end up with some sort of paper records or paper qualifications appropriate to their level of ability which they can present to their future employer who, it is naively assumed, will be there waiting to welcome them, and they will thus fit smoothly into the world that the adult perceives as given.

It was this perception that was challenged in the 1970s — the viewpoint that with continued technological and industrial advance, humankind's material provision and comforts could be increased indefinitely and that provided we all slotted in neatly we would all benefit, and that this was the proper aim of social progress, and therefore it was the proper aim of education to prepare us for our part in it. On the contrary, many people came to see that humankind's arrogant belief that it can mould the whole universe to suit its own purposes was an affront and an outrage to the natural world, and that it would inevitably bring its day of retribution, which suddenly appeared much closer than anyone had previously thought. And so came the idea of the sustainable planet where it would be accepted that the world is an intricate, mutually supportive network of living things in which we must respect not only all other human beings but all life, and that we must be restrained in our pursuit of the lion's share of resources.

'Alternative' education became a part of this mo
developed a marriage of A.S. Neill's idea (Neill, 196
whom freedom nurtures self-motivation and self-disc
'alternative' idea that freedom would release them from   ...ty to
an unjust and eventually self-destructive society.

In retrospect it is hardly surprising that this hybrid never got beyond the level of theory and fantasy, since there is indeed an incompatibility between an educational process which aims to encourage creativity, and the ruling educational hierarchy whose hidden curriculum is to maintain the stability of the status quo and subservience to authority. The alternative education movement was smothered and suppressed almost as it germinated.

THE SUPPRESSION OF ALTERNATIVES: A CASE STUDY

A scheme of HE mxed out.

If this sounds like one of those woolly assertions that are found on examination to be unsupported and unsupportable, here is an example of how this process of suppression operated.

In 1973–74 my wife and I were involved in a project in Yorkshire in which thirty 15/16-year-olds were taken out of school altogether for their last school year and worked on a project basis at a learning centre located within the community but right away from the school. The participants in this project were self-selected on a volunteer basis, at any rate in theory; in fact there may have been some restrictions on volunteering, since all who took part were under-achievers, and quite a few had records of truancy and disruptiveness in school. Throughout their year with the project, however, they led a generally active and purposeful life, attended fairly regularly, and showed many skills and aptitudes. In spite of poor school records (only one of them took any examination — a CSE in English, for which he obtained a Grade IV pass) many of them showed real intelligence, and in discussion they quickly became articulate, argumentative and lively-minded. Also, although initially there was some scepticism and suspicion among the local community, by the end of the scheme we had secured a great deal of co-operation and goodwill.

It is difficult to assess such a limited scheme over only two years, but at any rate by most of the usual educational criteria, with the exception of paper qualifications (which we never aimed for), it was a considerable

...nd created a lot of interest. Michael Duane, who monitored the ...t year of the scheme, wrote 'the transformation in the pupils' attitudes, their self-discipline, their self-confidence and their self-respect was quite remarkable.' (Duane and Webb, undated.)

Nevertheless, at the end of two years the scheme was terminated and as far as I am aware there have been no attempts to resuscitate it or replicate it elsewhere. Royston Lambert, at the time head of Dartington Hall School, who initiated the project, had written in his proposal: 'If the scheme shows elements of success, other similar or multi-age groups might hive off until whole networks of groups operate in the community' (Lambert, 1972) and it was certainly envisaged at the start that the project should be replicated. The reasons for its abrupt closure are not clear: the ostensible reason was economic, and it is difficult to challenge this in detail. However, in spite of some extravagance in staffing (pupils:staff ratio roughly 8:1) the project was not costly in relation to the large sums at that time allocated to education: there were substantial resources available for post-ROSLA projects from a variety of sources, especially of course those projects that had the support of the education authorities; it was a question of priorities.

The Yorkshire project attracted hostility from some members of the school staff, who apparently took exception to a scheme set up on their doorstep with children whom they regarded as 'their own', by a wealthy independent organisation (Dartington Hall), which by its success sharply questioned the adequacy of the provision made by the school and its staff; and the attitude of the school was supported by the LEA. Another possible reason is that this took place at the time of local authority reorganisation. The LEA which set up the scheme was the wealthy, liberal-minded West Riding; the LEA which scotched it was Doncaster Metropolitan Borough.

Whatever the reasons, and obviously they were complicated and multi-faceted, after two years the scheme was closed down and rather hastily buried; nothing has been heard of it since. This is merely an example of the way in which the established order, even at the lower end of the hierarchy, will suppress an initiative that challenges its basic assumptions. Education has never been in the vanguard of social change: it has always supported the social system and been its servant, and its progress will only follow and mirror social progress. The following exchange took place at a discussion in St Pancras Town Hall in 1971:

> 'But do you think, Ivan Illich, that your aim of deschooling society can take place unless major social, political and economic changes have already begun to take place in that society?'
> 'Certainly not; of course not.' *(Duane, undated.)*

The deschooling alternative

So we seem to be caught in a familiar ⸋
more appositely, we are caught up in a kn⸋
loosen it at one end the more we tighten the o⸋
strangled. Education will not change until socie⸋
not change until people change, and people will ⸋
education continues to mould them to conform. H⸋
process of change is not quite so constricted: progre⸋ ⸋y
and ineluctably determined by theory. Deschooling as I⸋ ⸋ged it
may still be far away, but the idea is not dead, and ed⸋ ⸋on out of
school is very much alive.

HOME-BASED EDUCATION

[handwritten: first caught attention ok]

In this country the legality of educating children out of school first
attracted wide public attention in the early 1960s as the result of a High
Court appeal by Mrs Joy Baker against Norfolk Education Authority, in
which she won the right to educate her children at home, and of the
book *Children in Chancery* (Hutchinson, 1964) which she wrote subsequently.

However, it was not until the mid-1970s that a number of people
began to follow her lead. When they did so, their methods and practices
bore little resemblance to the educational scenarios of Illich or other
'deschoolers': nearly all of them worked more or less in isolation within
their own homes. One reason for this isolation was the purely practical
one that not enough deschooling families lived in any one area to form
groups that could work together. This was compounded by an uncertainty about the legal position, and the saga of Mrs Baker's long and
harrowing fight with the authorities: it seemed safer to keep a low
profile and avoid anything which might provoke the authorities to
retaliate. For these reasons deschooling has tended to remain a private
activity, even though this withdrawal into the home seems to go against
the present-day trend to challenge the validity of the nuclear family
isolated from its neighbours and from the community, and of the mother
as the person tied to the home with her brood of children. *[handwritten: start of EO]*

There are many examples of families whose concern for their children
and balanced relationship with them produce admirable results, but
there are others which present a spectacle of mild suffocation. Janov,
the American psychologist, lists a 'host of neurotic reasons for having
children, none of which have to do with producing a new human being
on this earth' (Janov, 1977), and one cannot help feeling that many of

: lists, for example 'to produce someone who will be someone the parent can have all to himself', parallel the reasons some parents wishing to keep their children out of school and create a situation where the child is 'smothered with love and care'.

In some cases this can produce an oppression from which an escape to school may be the lesser of two evils. However oppressive a child finds his or her school, there is usually some opportunity for rebellion, revolution or evasion, which may be quite a healthy, exciting and positive reaction; but challenging oppression within the family will always be likely to leave a residue of guilt and to create neuroses which perpetuate the neuroses of the parents.

Royston Lambert in setting out his proposal for the Yorkshire deschooling project lists nine 'principles and approaches'. The first three of these are:

1. Young people need the continuous and sympathetic support and guidance of an adult (or adults) other than their parents.
2. Children need a base other than home from which to operate.
3. Most young people develop beneficially by interaction within a group or groups of other young people but need not be exclusively confined to this age texture. *(Lambert, 1972)*

Lambert recognised that one essential requirement of any deschooling scheme is that it does not expose the children to continuous and exclusive surveillance from the parents and the home. In theory these requirements can be provided either at school or in the home, but in practice it is rather difficult to achieve either way. In the former, children can rarely identify sufficiently with the school to feel that it provides them and their groups with a secure 'operational base', and the adults associated with the school are bound to feel they must support the authority of the school, and will be seen as having this role. It is possible for a teacher to establish him or herself as being 'on the children's side', and this certainly sometimes occurs, but it is a difficult tightrope for a teacher to tread without divided loyalties and in the end an unenviable reputation for bad faith.

Equally, home education can provide these needs, and some families succeed in doing so, but it is difficult to create a degree of independence that is going to release the child from a feeling of parental pressure and supervision. It is important to emphasise that what is being referred to here is not a matter of failure or inadequacy on the part of the parents or children: it can occur with the most caring and conscientious parents, the most amenable and loving children, the (by outward appearances) most benign family situation. It is a psychological interaction inherent in the parent/child relationship and is largely unconscious and undetected.

EDUCATION OTHERWISE

Some of those who were practising, or interested i̶
school came together in 1975–76 to exchange view
Education Otherwise was born in 1977, as a membe̶ꞏ
whose principal aim was to provide a support, advice a̶ ꞏꞏꞏꞏꞏmation
network for such families. The membership rose steadily but slowly to
about 500 at the beginning of 1982 and then much faster to 900 by the
end of 1982. It is now (mid-1983) over 1000, and interest in education
out of school continues to grow both among the general public and
within the media.

A statement of the aims and objectives of Education Otherwise was
agreed in 1978, and the following is a shortened summary of them:

1. To reaffirm that parents have the primary responsibility for their
    children's education and that they have the right to exercise this
    responsibility by educating them out of school.
2. To establish the primary right of children that full consideration,
    with due allowance for their age and understanding, shall be
    given to their wishes and feelings regarding their education.
3. To support families in which for any good reason a child is being
    educated out of school, particularly:
    (a) by disseminating information and advice through the
         medium of a newsletter, booklets, and in other ways;
    (b) by providing specific legal help;
    (c) by arranging meetings and by supporting the formation of
         local groups.
4. To support families where a child is suffering educationally,
    socially or emotionally from compulsory school attendance.

The statement also affirmed that it was not the group's intention to act
in conflict with schools or education authorities, and that it endorsed the
legal responsibilities of the authorities as a safeguard for children who
might otherwise be deprived of their right to education, and as providers
of educational resources and services.

The first thing to note in this statement is that Education Otherwise
did not commit itself to any agreed ideology of education. This was not
because we were undecided or could not reach agreement, but because
we did not address ourselves to the problem, and did not consider this to
be our role. Of course, ideas abounded and still abound and are
exchanged through meetings, newsletters and other publications, but
there is no consistency in what is practised by families. As Ian Lister has
put it, 'De-schooling is a rag-bag, full of fine bits and pieces' (Lister,
1971).

...tion Otherwise's concern is with the issue of human rights: the ...ly's right to choose its own style of education and to put it into practice in whatever way it believes to be right. We are thus absolutely opposed to compulsory schooling, but not to schooling itself: we recognise that, given a free choice, school is at present what most families will opt for. Equally, we do not believe that the education authorities should have the power to direct what sort of education we provide (any more than that there should be a Ministry of Child Nutrition to direct what food we provide, or a Department of Accoutrements to supervise what clothes we provide) but we accept the need for the authorities to act as a 'safeguard for children who might otherwise be deprived of their right to education'.

In the second place, partly because education is legally the responsibility of the parent, Education Otherwise is addressed to parents, and the children for whose benefit the organisation exists do not have much of a voice in its affairs. For example, there is a group concerned with the interests of Education Otherwise families who have children with disabilities, and there is now mooted a group for one-parent families, but there is no group of Education Otherwise children whose aim is to voice their needs and interests. This omission does not indicate a plot to suppress their views, but it does, I think, suggest that there is an unacknowledged and perhaps unconscious assumption among Education Otherwise families that the parent can always speak for the child — an assumption that would not survive the most cursory observation of reality. Thus we have not tackled the prickly issue of how the phrase 'full consideration . . . to their wishes and feelings' is to be interpreted in practice: how full is 'full consideration' when the child's wishes conflict with those of the parents? How much allowance is 'due' to 5-year-olds or 10-year-olds if the parents in their adult wisdom do not consider their children's wishes and feelings wise or mature? Children's opportunity to make their own choices or even to express their genuine opinions rests entirely with the individual family. Education Otherwise has not yet given any thought to creating a channel of communication or support which would help children in bad family situations.

Third, the statement does not express any concern about the wider social consequences of what it sees as the failure of schooling, by for example campaigning for a new approach to education, or committing itself to community deschooling on the Illich pattern. The nearest it gets to this is the support it promises in the formation of local groups and meetings. Attempts have in fact been made to set up cohesive local groups but they haven't met with much success and have usually limited themselves to occasional get-togethers among families in one vicinity, and have not established very much interaction with the local neighbourhood. It is evident that whatever the intentions of the founders of Education Otherwise, the movement has not become an ardent advocate of Illich and the earlier deschoolers. It derives its ideas much more from John Holt (Holt, 1981) and A.S. Neill (Neill, 1968) (though the writer of 'There are no problem children: only problem parents' and 'Most of my work seems to consist of correcting parental mistakes' would hardly have been a keen supporter of the spread of home education).

It is right that, as a membership organisation, Education Otherwise should serve its members and that this should be its primary aim, for it is from its loyal and swelling membership that its credibility derives. But this has meant that it has not yet fostered the sort of educational scenario which would be open to a whole community that was being envisaged ten years ago, and has not seriously attempted to do so.

For example, in places where the education authority has closed the local school an opportunity has been created for some sort of community deschooling alternative, but although the idea has been mooted and even occasionally put into practice temporarily as a form of protest or pressure on the authority, there has never been sufficient dynamism to get such a scheme off the ground permanently.

The last paragraph in the Education Otherwise statement of aims runs: 'We envisage a situation in which school and other educational services provide a resource that is freely available to all members of the community, whatever their age'. This was a carefully-thought-out statement, pregnant with potential, but no significant steps in that direction have yet been achieved or attempted. It is possible that with Education Otherwise's increasing membership some sort of community schooling may become more practicable, but even when there has been a reasonable density of families in one area they have found it very difficult to co-operate, and attempts to do so tend to be torpedoed by differences of approach and consequent disagreement. The sort of qualities of energy and independence that are required to reject conventional wisdom and launch out on one's own too often coincide with strong opinions and an obstinate attachment to one's own viewpoint that obstructs co-operation.

To summarise, deschooling as practised in this country does provide an opportunity for many positive individual approaches to upbringing and education, and in addition a very necessary, though limited, channel of escape from unsatisfactory and often intolerable school situations, but it has its own dangers; it also has its limitations, for it is a demanding option which a majority of families hesitate to tackle. Those prepared to do so must possess a lot of energy and have confidence in their abilities and skills, and they must enjoy the company of their children to the exclusion of many other interests; and in present-day society the main load will normally fall upon the woman.

It is probable that this style of deschooling will never appeal to more than a minority of families, most of whom will belong to the privileged sector of society. It is not surprising that in many eyes deschooling is viewed with much the same suspicion as is directed towards private education. Education Otherwise has deliberately chosen a limited role, of servicing the rights of a minority group, but in doing so it has fulfilled the valuable function of keeping the doors open: an increasing number of families have asserted the right to practise deschooling, there is a growing body of deschoolers, and there is a widening experience of their opportunities, problems and successes.

It is perhaps just because it has this simple, clear-cut, definable and practical aim that Education Otherwise has emerged as a thriving organisation from the mêlée of the 1970s.

CONCLUSION

What then of the future? Two questions remain in the context of this short paper: what, after ten years, remains of the concept of a deschooled society, and what role have present deschoolers, and in particular Education Otherwise, to play in it?

A.K. Green, criticising Illich, says, 'There is an inadequacy, if not a total lack, of supportive documentation for most of his claims' and 'There is no evidence that de-schooling provides all the solutions' (Green, undated). This is true: deschooling on the 1970s model is a hypothesis; it has not been tested at the bar of experience, at least not in this country. It is, however, a possible course and one that demands to be tested. Is it right, though, to use children as the subjects, and perhaps victims, of hypothetical experiments? Many people claim that to do so is to treat them as no more than guinea-pigs. What seems to be over-looked is that all education treats children as guinea-pigs, as the victims of experimental situations, for there is no agreement about either education's end product or its processes.

Is the purpose of education to mould children like pots or to fertilise them like gardens? Is it to 'initiate them into worthwhile activities' (Peters, 1966), and if so, what are worthwhile activities and by what criteria is their worth assessed? Is it 'concerned with reason and intelligence' (Bell and Grant, 1974), or is it 'an openness to one's environment which is a continuous process in a healthy life' (Mother-

son, undated)? Is it to 'subvert attitudes, beliefs and assump.
foster chaos and uselessness' (Postman and Weingartner, 1971) c.
'concerned only with the present lives of children' (Dennison, 1972)'.
it 'the exercise of creative skills, the competence to undertake and
complete tasks, and the ability to cope with everyday life, doing all these
things in co-operation with others' (Manifesto of 'Education for Capability', 1982)?

'Everyone has a right to Education', states the United Nations
Declaration of Human Rights, and it 'shall be directed to the full
development of the human personality', and then it leaves it at that. In
the UK it must be 'efficient, and suitable to the child's age, ability and
aptitude', but there is nowhere a hint on how to interpret these
high-sounding but fuzzy phrases. Suitable for what? Suitable for the 'full
development of the human personality' — but what is the personality
and how does one develop it? Whatever it is, education is presumably
intended as a preparation for life in twentieth-century society — but
what sort of life, and what sort of society? And what about twenty-first-
century society?

Professor Sugarman, of the University of California, has summed it
up: 'There is no social consensus over what are the proper goals and
means of education . . . If both are indeterminate, what is one to do?'
(Sugarman, 1979). What indeed? The same could be said of life, and the
answer there seems to be that in a democratic, libertarian society we do
what we like, within certain limits of social acceptability and responsibility. It is this freedom of choice, we believe, that makes life worth while,
and that is our guarantee of a stable social order and a steady
evolutionary adaptability and development towards new and better
social orders.

I would assert that education requires a similar diversity of approach
and for similar reasons, and that rather than aiming to supersede the
present system with some different and better system, we should make
possible and encourage a great variety of systems, a diversity of
provisions.

What, then, is to be done here and now? Recently some Government
spokespeople have made tentative suggestions that Government plans
for privatisation could involve a loosening of restrictions which would be
favourable to alternative education. Both the voucher system and small,
parent-based schools on the Danish model might provide an opportunity and stimulus for new alternative initiatives. Naturally they must be
looked upon with great suspicion and many reservations, as part of the
Government's plans to open education to market forces, which can only
be seen to benefit still further the well-to-do at the expense of the
original aim of state education, which was to provide free education for

...ome. The fact that state education favours the ...nd indeed can be seen as a form of discriminative ...poor, is not likely to lessen this suspicion. But even ...reactionary and destructive step for the future of ...have to be accepted as a fait accompli. It may happen, ...ere could be a case for taking advantage of its positive side. This ... a matter for individual judgement and principles, and will not be an easy decision. The alternative movement has always been very vulnerable to accusations that it is politically besmirched, and a transition from being 'pink, wishy-washy, middle-class anarcho-liberals' to being 'true-blue, upper-class, anarcho-tories' may be difficult to face; I think it will take a lot of clear thinking to grasp the underlying issues. Colin Ward writes: 'The teaching profession wants to eliminate the "private sector" while I see it as the one guarantee that genuine radical experiment can happen' (Ward, 1982). I think we must accept a lead from this courageous statement by our leading theoretical anarchist.

It is possible that Education Otherwise's first six years have been ones of cautious, embryonic growth which has necessarily taken place within the protective walls of the family, and that it is too early to assess where it will move in the future; it has now reached a stage in its maturation at which it could have the confidence to move outwards and interact with the wider community. It is the fact that it has not hoisted its flag on the flagpole of any transitory educational theory which gives it its opportunity. Its strength is its lack of an educational ideology, its commitment to diversity. It is the only educational movement which is not saddled with some ephemeral theoretical base and which nevertheless has the credibility, deriving mainly from its rapidly growing membership, to voice a genuinely radical challenge to the present system. If it were to move out from its present introspection and grasp this opportunity it could assume the leadership of a wider movement. Such a change of direction, together with a new flexibility arising from privatisation, an increasing number of school closures, and a despairing reaction to the declining provision of state education, could lead to new opportunities for alternative education within the present decade.

REFERENCES

Bell, R. and Grant, N. (1974) *A Mythology of British Education*. St Albans: Panther.

Dennison, G. (1972) *Lives of Children*. Harmondsworth: Penguin.

Duane, M. *Education For What.* Published by the author.

Duane, M. and Webb, E. *Dialogues of Experience,* in transcript, Garnett College, London.

Friere, P. (1972) *Pedagogy of the Oppressed.* Harmondsworth: Penguin.

Goodman, P. (1956) *Growing Up Absurd.* New York: Random House.

Goodman, P. (1971) *Compulsory Miseducation.* Harmondsworth: Penguin.

Green, A.K. *Deschooling: An Alternative Route.* Unpublished paper, University of York.

Holt, J. (1969) *How Children Fail.* Harmondsworth: Penguin.

Holt, J. (1970) *How Children Learn.* Harmondsworth: Penguin.

Holt, J. (1977) *Instead of Education.* Harmondsworth: Penguin.

Holt, J. (1981) *Teach Your Own.* Brightlingsea: Lighthouse Books.

Illich, I. (1971) *Deschooling Society.* Harmondsworth: Penguin.

Illich, I. (1974) *After Deschooling — What?* London: Writers and Readers Publishing Co-op.

Janov, A. (1977) *The Feeling Child.* London: Sphere.

Lambert, R. (1972) *Alternatives to School.* Exeter: University of Exeter.

Lister, I. (1971) Introduction to Illich, I. *Deschooling Society.* Harmondsworth: Penguin.

Lister, I. (1974) *De-schooling: A reader.* Cambridge: Cambridge University Press.

Manifesto of 'Education for Capability' (1982), Royal Society of Arts.

Motherson, K. *The Great Brain Robbery.* Published by the author as Moss Side Press.

Neill, A.S. (1968) *Summerhill.* Harmondsworth: Penguin.

Peters, R.S. (1966) *Ethics and Education.* London: George Allen & Unwin.

Postman, N. and Weingartner, C. (1971) *Teaching As A Subversive Activity.* Harmondsworth: Penguin.

Reimer, E. (1971) *School is Dead.* Harmondsworth: Penguin.

Stallibrass, A. (1977) *The Self-Respecting Child.* London: Thames and Hudson.

Sugarman, S. (1979) Freedom and choice in the family, *Where,* April.

Ward, C. (1982) *Anarchy in Action.* Freedom Press.

10

'Parents and children': 100 years of the Parents' National Educational Union and its World-wide Education Service

Hugh Boulter

INTRODUCTION

'Children are born persons.' So wrote Charlotte Mason some 100 years ago (Mason, 1925). It is the starting point for her thinking and is the basis of the work which is still carried on by the World-wide Education Service (WES) of the Parents' National Educational Union (PNEU). However, this insistence that children should be treated as individuals is not a sentimental version of 'child-centred' education, but rather an honest realisation that each child is different, with varying talents, needs and interests. It militates healthily against dogmatism in education, and it has enabled the PNEU to be involved with both home schooling and ordinary schooling throughout its history. In this it is perhaps unique, as in so many other ways. While the great majority of children will, and should, continue in ordinary schools, nevertheless for some children in certain circumstances home schooling is clearly the most satisfactory alternative. The most obvious reason is remoteness. WES has families in over 120 countries, many of them living in very isolated places, while some are on boats sailing round the world. Another reason is special educational needs, e.g. haemophilia, dyslexia or Down's syndrome, and yet another is quite simply that some parents feel they can do a better educational job than the schools which are available. We have an increasing number of families in the United Kingdom, to whom I shall return later, but it should be made quite clear from the outset that the PNEU has little patience either with the arid, defensive professionalism of a minority of teachers who think that they alone can educate children or with those parents who seem to be opposed to all schools per se.

118

CHARLOTTE MASON AND THE HOME-SCHOOL SERVICE

In this chapter I propose first of all to outline the history of the PNEU movement and the services which are offered by WES, and then to give some indication of the educational thinking which lies behind it. It relies heavily on a recently published pamphlet, *The Philosophy of Charlotte Mason in the 1980s* (Boulter, 1983).

The PNEU stems from the pioneering work of Charlotte Mason, the late Victorian educationist. She wrote a number of influential books including *Home Education* (Mason, 1896), *Parents and Children* (Mason, 1897) and *An Essay Towards a Philosophy of Education* (Mason, 1925). In 1890 she launched and for many years edited a new journal, *The Parents' Review* (Mason, 1890), which is still produced three times a year as the *Journal of the World-wide Education Service of the PNEU* (Boulter, 1980). In 1891 she opened the House of Education to train young women to become governesses and teachers: it still remains as the Charlotte Mason College, Ambleside, and is a college of education administered by Cumbria County Council, but it no longer produces Charlotte Mason trained teachers as such (CMTs, as they style themselves). The Parents' National Educational Union itself was founded in 1890. It had branches all over the country, and indeed all over the world, and was active in encouraging parents to become involved in their own children's education. So, for example, in 1902 there were requests to set up some twenty new branches in places as far apart as Bradford, Brisbane, Copenhagen, Dublin and Swansea. Interestingly, it is this aspect of the organisation which alone has atrophied: almost every other aspect has developed and can be seen in the work of WES today.

From the training of governesses at the House of Education has developed the Home-School Service, which is perhaps the aspect of the PNEU's work for which it is best known. The two essentials of this service are the programmes and the tutors. It is not a correspondence course in the correct sense of the phrase: it depends upon involving the parents (or governesses!) in the education of the child and giving them the support which they need in order to perform their task effectively. Ideally the families come into the WES headquarters, where they are seen by a tutor who will assess the child's needs and capabilities, and adjust the programmes accordingly. WES operates as a bookseller in its own right and holds in stock all the books that it recommends. It is therefore possible for a family to come in, be seen by their tutor and be provided with all the necessary books and equipment within 24 hours. The families are then encouraged to write to their tutor as often as they wish and to send in an assessment of the child's work at least every term. The tutors are all qualified and experienced teachers who are able to reassure parents about the quality and level of their children's work. Obviously it is different from ordinary schooling, but it can be extremely effective. It does depend on a reasonable emotional relationship between parent and child and on a degree of self-discipline — what Charlotte Mason would have called the 'discipline of habit' (Mason, 1896); it also requires a certain educational standard of the parent, but this is often less important than the other two factors. One mother overcame the conflict of roles between parent and teacher by getting her daughter to leave the house at 9 a.m. 'Bye-bye, Mummy,' said the little girl, who then walked round the block, knocked on the door, and when her mother opened it said 'Good morning, Mrs Gilmore'. Lessons then started, with mother happily ensconced in the role of teacher.

The programmes are the schemes of work which are supplied to parents. They have recently been revised to ensure that the materials which are recommended are the best currently available in the United Kingdom. They explain to parents how to set up and run a home-school using the books and materials supplied by the WES. Many families are understandably concerned that the courses should be comparable to the work done in ordinary schools. It is therefore a great reassurance to them and to us that the Department of Education and Science was prepared to give them their endorsement:

> . . . we are satisfied that the programmes of the World-wide Education Service if followed conscientiously, can be used to provide children with an education which would help them subsequently to fit into schools in this country at the appropriate level. *(WES, 1983)*

It should be noted that the great majority of children following WES home-school courses are in the age range 5 to 13. However, a small number of less academic pupils stay with us above that age and we are looking at developing more pre-school materials to meet the needs of both individual children and nursery groups. Another aspect which should be mentioned is the increasing demand for supplementary material. In fact the WES programmes are designed to be used as a whole and are in accord with one of Charlotte Mason's tenets that children should have a broad curriculum. However, we have always been happy to provide single subjects. For example, several children outside the United Kingdom attend non-English-speaking schools and therefore follow our English course as a special subject at home. Others do mathematics, science, history and geography as well as French and Latin where those subjects are not covered by the school or where the parents consider the school teaches them inadequately. In a few instances parents follow the complete WES course with their children even when they are in ordinary schools. This makes for a long day and is very tiring, so in general is not to be encouraged. In addition to the single subjects, however, there is an increasing demand to provide material which supplements rather than replaces other material. Although it is not our prime intention to meet this market, nevertheless much of the new material can justifiably be used in this way. Thus we have recently produced an environmental science folder entitled *Starting from a Walk* (Wilson, 1983) which takes the Charlotte Mason idea of a nature walk and adapts it so that it can be used anywhere in the world. It consists of some 80 themes or topics covering the main aspects of environmental science. A further example is our new astronomy cassette with accompanying notes which, although designed to be used largely in the Northern Hemisphere, can be used south of the Equator as well. A third example is our collaboration with the National Gallery. Picture study has long been a particular aspect of the PNEU curriculum and many former pupils recall with affection the specially produced Medici monographs on famous painters. These, sadly, are now out of print and stocks are dwindling, so we have developed with the Education Officer at the National Gallery a series of themes and topics based on their recent publication *100 Great Paintings: Duccio to Picasso* (Gordon, 1981). It follows many of the ideas developed by the National Gallery for holiday activities for children.

INVOLVEMENT WITH SCHOOLS

I have dwelt at length on the Home-School aspect of the WES/PNEU services, since it is the one which is most germane to a book on alternative educational futures. However, in order to complete the picture, mention should also be made of other aspects of the organisation's work. There has always been an involvement with schools. In the United Kingdom today there are some thirty PNEU schools affiliated to the parent organisation. Typically they are girls' independent day preparatory schools. They receive copies of all material produced by WES/PNEU and are invited to an annual conference for head teachers and their staff. In general they are sympathetic to the ideas and practices of Charlotte Mason. An increasing aspect of the work, however, has been the Advisory Service, through which WES helps to establish and run schools overseas for British communities and for companies employing British personnel. Advice can be given from an early stage on school design, schedules of furniture, materials and equipment, the supply of books, and the recruitment of teaching staff. Then, once the school is established, WES will monitor standards by paying regular advisory visits and, in the case of smaller schools, also by scrutinising samples of pupils' work. The development of advisory visits has led inevitably to an increase in travel by WES staff, which in turn has given them an opportunity to talk to other potential clients and to existing British-style schools. As a result of this WES is increasingly becoming involved in providing in-service training, educational advice and inspection services to British-style schools overseas.

This involvement of WES both with home-schools and with British-style schools outside the United Kingdom has led to the development of the Counselling Service, through which WES will help both individual and corporate clients with educational advice. The PNEU has traditionally been associated with both the maintained and the independent sectors of education, so WES is uniquely placed to give advice on a wide range of educational matters. This advice can range from a discussion of the educational options available to families returning to the United Kingdom, to assessment by our own educational psychologist of pupils with special needs. It covers advice on educational policy for companies starting to work abroad and includes such matters as salary levels and conditions of service for teachers.

The outcome of these developments is that WES/PNEU is probably the only organisation the main function of which is to meet the educational needs of British expatriates. However, having said that, there is no doubt that the demand for the Home-School service in the United Kingdom is growing. The policy of the PNEU's Council of Management is quite clear on this: the vast majority of children will continue to, and should, attend normal schools. However, where parents wish to educate their own children at home we consider that it is nearly always preferable that they follow a recognised course such as our own rather than try to do it themselves. We certainly do not wish to challenge the work of either maintained or independent schools, so our attitude tends to be cautious. The outcome is that families who do decide to use our materials are rarely challenged by the local education authorities, which of course have a responsibility for ensuring that the education provided by parents is efficient.

At this stage I should perhaps say something about the organisation of WES/PNEU itself. The PNEU is an educational charity and a company limited by guarantee; it is therefore non-profit-making. However, it receives grants or assistance from no outside source, so it has to make charges to cover its costs. Some six years ago it was decided to operate largely under the title 'The World-wide Education Service'; this was felt not only to be more self-explanatory but also to emphasise the genuinely world-wide nature of the organisation. It is governed by a council, all the members of which give their services voluntarily and on which are represented various aspects of education, the professions and commerce. In addition there are two assessors: one a staff inspector at the Department of Education and Science, the other the Chief Education Adviser to a local education authority. The presidents are the Countess Mountbatten of Burma and her husband, Lord Brabourne.

THE PHILOSOPHY OF CHARLOTTE MASON

Having looked in some detail at the present position of WES/PNEU, it is now time to examine more closely the philosophy of Charlotte Mason, which has underpinned and inspired this work for nearly 100 years. What emerges strongly is the abiding soundness of her ideas. Their application, of course, has changed and much of her terminology is unfamiliar. Nevertheless, they do merit restatement, and six interrelated strands can be identified: the individuality of children, a structured syllabus, a wide curriculum, a stimulating and enjoyable atmosphere, the role of the teacher, and the role of the parent.

A structured syllabus

The emphasis on the individuality of children has already been touched upon and I do not need to labour its importance: it is likely to meet with general support, especially in alternative education circles. More controversial in this context is the stress on a structured syllabus. As will be seen below, this does not mean a rigid curriculum, but it is an attempt to ensure that children are introduced to a wide range of knowledge and experience: their learning is therefore not dictated solely by their parents' background or the environment in which they find themselves. Traditionally the structure has been provided in WES/PNEU circles by the programmes. Most home-school families start by following the programmes fairly closely, as they need the support which the structure provides. However, as they gain confidence they are encouraged to branch out in ways that follow the interests of the children and fit the particular circumstances in which they find themselves. Schools even more will wish to, and should, develop their own lines of work. Nevertheless, the programmes remain a useful framework delineating the main areas of a broad curriculum and are there to provide detailed guidance in areas where teachers feel less confident. The important point is that there should be a clearly defined curriculum.

A wide curriculum

The third strand is the need for a wide curriculum: not that the 'three Rs' should be abandoned, but they can only be developed fully by their application to a wide range of studies. This broad curriculum is based not only on content but also on first-hand experience and the acquisition of sound language skills: listening, speaking, reading and writing. Indeed it is interesting that 'narration', one of Charlotte Mason's distinctive contributions to educational practice, is an attempt to develop listening and speaking skills in a way which is all too often neglected nowadays. This is not the place to discuss 'narration' in great detail, but a brief outline will give some indication of what it involves. The parent or teacher gives the background to a selected passage which is then read aloud without interruption. The child or children then retell the passage in their own words covering the salient points. Then follows discussion or practical work. There are many variations encompassing group work, drama, written work and art, but the essence is listening with understanding, assimilating the material and thinking about it. Charlotte Mason's emphasis on reading and writing is less remarkable, although she would surely have supported both the involvement of parents and the use of a range of approaches to ensure reading for understanding. Parents have an important part to play here, partly because their involvement and support are a great encouragement to their children but also because in a busy classroom no teacher has as much time to devote to each individual as might be wished. It is hardly surprising that in our home-schools, where parent and teacher are the same person, children rarely fail to become both articulate and fluent readers at an early stage.

If the acquisition of language skills is the starting point for the broad curriculum, the next step is the need to draw upon the child's surroundings and practical experience. Nowhere is this more true than in mathematics, where Charlotte Mason recognised what is now generally accepted: that practical experience is essential to back up mathematical concepts. It is the application of mathematics to concrete situations which is important: the acquisition of computational skills is fundamental and thus a basis on which more advanced mathematics work can be built. However, perhaps more original in her day was her emphasis on practical experience as a basis for science and the study of the environment, e.g. 'patient, unflagging day-by-day observation and recording what he has already seen for himself. We must not confound a glib knowledge of scientific textbooks with the patient investigation carried out by ourselves' (Mander, undated). It is against this background that we should see another of Charlotte Mason's distinctive educational practices, the nature notebook. Here was an opportunity for children and students to observe the habitat around them (whether urban or rural), to record, to hypothesise and to draw conclusions. Here indeed was an 'integrated' approach: not only did accurate observation form a valid basis for scientific inquiry, it encouraged writing skills, statistical skills and, perhaps most markedly, artistic skills — some of the nature notebooks from the early part of the century show a facility in water-colour painting which is rarely seen in schools and colleges today. An added advantage of this approach for WES/PNEU is that so many families and schools are overseas. It is therefore an opportunity for children in such widely different environments as Saudi Arabia and Indonesia to make regular observations and recordings of what is around them: the soil and the night sky, as well as the flora and fauna.

Similarly, in history and geography (the humanities) it is important to move from the known to the unknown where possible. Again, our families overseas have a tremendous advantage in being able to experience the geography of different countries at first hand. There is therefore emphasis not only on the need to understand one's own culture but also to learn about other cultures with tolerance and understanding, but not uncritically; Charlotte Mason certainly saw the study of history as a means of encouraging children to make judgements about people and the consequences of their actions. She believed firmly in the importance of source material: that children should be encouraged to visit museums and 'The child should get his first notions of a given period . . . from the original sources of history, the writings of contemporaries' (Mander, undated).

However, particularly overseas, it is important not only to develop history and geography from the local situation, but also to instil in children an awareness of their 'own' culture which may actually be little known to them. They have a need for 'roots', which will include a knowledge of their country's history based on a grasp of its basic chronology as well as a knowledge of their country's geography. This in turn can be linked with other aspects such as music and picture study. In a multinational context such an approach has widespread and challenging implications.

The acquisition of language skills and the encouragement of practical experience are the bases for a wide curriculum which nowadays is generally accepted as good educational practice — another example of Charlotte Mason's far-sightedness.

Before going into this in some detail, this may be a convenient place to mention the Christian basis of Charlotte Mason's thinking; she saw this as the fount of all her educational philosophy. Both her concern for the individual child and the inspirational nature of learning ('education is the spirit') derive from her Christian belief, and traditionally the PNEU day began with Bible study which, as has already been mentioned, was often linked to narration based on a good modern translation. Times, however, have changed: not only are many parents avowedly agnostic or atheist, but an increasing number of our families are members of different faiths. In these circumstances it must be up to individual families or teachers in schools to do what they feel is appropriate. However, there are two aspects of Charlotte Mason's thought on religious education which deserve emphasis and which exemplify her wider thinking: first, the understanding of Christianity should be based on a study of the Bible and not some 'watered down' version; second, we should never underestimate the child's capacity for religious understanding.

To return to the main issue of the wide curriculum, mention has already been made of language skills, mathematics, science, history and geography; now we need to turn our attention to picture study, music appreciation, civics and foreign languages. Picture study, of course, is another hallmark of the PNEU movement and is often the one thing which former pupils remember as being most distinctive. Again, it is symptomatic of Charlotte Mason's thinking that she was anxious that children should be brought into touch with what was best in its field. Unfortunately, not everyone could have the work of great masters in their homes, and not everyone had ready access to art galleries, although that was to be encouraged, so she adopted the use of the next best thing: good-quality reproductions. The emphasis is on observation of content, line and colour, and on familiarity with specific painters and styles, and it is from this observation that not only appreciation but also the child's own work stems. As we have seen, it is a similar emphasis on observation in the nature notebooks which leads to high-quality water-colours of flowers and animals.

Similarly with music appreciation: Charlotte Mason was anxious that children should have access to the work of the greatest composers, and nowadays, with high-quality sound reproduction, this is even easier than in her day.

It should not be thought, however, that the PNEU movement has merely stood for a highly refined version of British culture. Apart from anything else, Charlotte Mason was anxious that her ideas should be applied to all levels of society: she was elitist merely in the sense that she felt that only the best was good enough for all children. Nevertheless, as has already been mentioned, she was also anxious that children should have a sympathetic understanding of other societies. To this end she was keen that children should learn a foreign language from an early age. In the United Kingdom this has tended to be French, but overseas it might be the local language of the country in which families find themselves. Several WES/PNEU children are in fact bilingual from an early age.

Children should also have a clear understanding of the workings of their own society and, although it is a subject which has tended to lapse, it is interesting to note that Charlotte Mason advocated the teaching of citizenship: ' . . . they are enabled to answer — "What do you know of (a) County Councils (b) District Councils (c) Parish Councils?"' (Mason, 1925). Children should therefore be aware of current affairs, both local and international, which in a sense brings us full circle: it has always been the aim of the PNEU movement to adapt the curriculum to the needs of a changing society so that children can play a constructive part in that society. It is therefore important that they should know not only how it works but also how it is changing. Thus, who can doubt that the computer will have a lasting impact on our lives? And it is surely significant that in many schools where teachers regard new technology with grave suspicion, albeit unadmitted, from an early age children are anxious to experiment with micro-processors and put them to their use.

Education is an atmosphere

Inevitably the third strand, the wide curriculum, takes some space to elucidate. The fourth strand, although shorter, is no less important: learning should be fun — 'education is an atmosphere' (Mason, 1925). Given an awareness of the individual child and a rich curriculum, education should be enjoyable. The two questions of competition and discipline also have a bearing on this. Charlotte Mason recognised that competition between children can be destructive; instead she emphasised the need for each child to compete against him or herself. As to discipline, great emphasis is laid on the need to provide plenty of interesting material for children to be absorbed in, and on a framework of self-discipline within which learning can take place — 'the discipline of habit' (Mason, 1896), including habits of concentration, attention, careful work and courtesy.

Teaching

The fifth and sixth strands concern the role of the parent and the teacher. I shall take them together as, of course, in WES terms they are often embodied in the same person in the home-school. Charlotte Mason refers to 'masterly inactivity' (Mander, undated). By this she does not mean that the teacher does nothing, but rather that he or she should not interfere or interrupt needlessly, or presuppose what will emerge. Having provided the necessary raw materials and encouraged the innate enthusiasm, the teacher should leave the child to produce his or her own work, not an aping of the teacher's ideas. Indeed, the very presence of the teacher provides a control even though he or she appears to do nothing. However, where the parent is not the teacher, as of course is the usual school situation, then the involvement of the parent in the educational process is invaluable, as Charlotte Mason realised. Schools have paid lip-service to this idea, but all too rarely act upon it, although it is a feature of many PNEU and WES schools that they draw upon the abilities of the parents, whether these be manual, professional or intellectual. The parent certainly has an important, although less central, role to play: for younger children, reading stories and listening to them being read; for all children, talking intelligently and interestedly about what they do at school. If the parents have worries then they should share them with teachers. Support should be given to school policy about homework and sensible habits of going to bed, watching television or video, etc., should be encouraged. Above all the relationship should be one of partnership so that each supports the other. In order to achieve this there must be easy means of communication, which can be encouraged in a variety of ways. Perhaps more than anything else a relaxed, friendly atmosphere is encouraging to parents as well as to children. They are made to feel welcome so that not only can anxieties be shared but offers of help accepted. Sometimes this will mean assisting during the school day as voluntary helpers or providing a particular skill or experience which the teaching staff do not possess. For example, in some schools parents of different faiths talk to the children about what they believe and about their religious practices. As there must be respect for the child, so also there must be mutual respect between parent and teacher.

In conclusion it may be said that Charlotte Mason's philosophy has stood the test of time not only in the sense that much of what she said has been absorbed into the best of current educational thinking, but also in that the organisation which she founded has been able to adapt to meet changing circumstances while remaining true to her ideals. Above all, her insistence on the importance and worth of the individual child has led to a pragmatic and non-dogmatic approach to education which welcomes variety and choice among educational alternatives. It is therefore uniquely able to contribute to home-schooling and ordinary schooling, to maintained education and independent education, without (we hope) becoming bland or indeterminate.

In the light of the current position of WES and the philosophical basis provided by Charlotte Mason, it may be helpful finally to see what developments can be foreseen for the future. It has already been shown that an emphasis on the individuality of the child leads to a non-dogmatic approach: what is suitable for one will not necessarily be suitable for another. The logical conclusion is therefore an emphasis on variety both within and between the independent and the maintained sectors of education so that parents may choose what is the best alternative available to them for their particular child. Among these alternatives is likely to be an increasing use of home-schools in which parents educate their own children. It has already been shown that this can be extremely effective, particularly when it can be supported by help from without. There really is no good reason in principle why the concept of 'flexischooling' outlined by Meighan in Chapter 12 should not be applied throughout the whole of the age range during which people receive education (i.e. from three years of age onwards). Certainly there is likely to be an increased emphasis on the involvement of parents in their children's education. Not only is this likely to be effective in itself in the sense that the children's education will benefit, but experience in general shows that where parents are involved in schools the standing of the teachers tends to be enhanced, and parents begin to understand just how difficult it is to organise and teach a group of twenty or more children all at the same time. If this mutual trust could be developed between the various partners in the educational process it could be of enormous benefit to the pupils and to the education system as a whole.

REFERENCES

Boulter, H.J. (ed.) (1980 onwards) *Journal of the World-wide Education Service of the PNEU.*

Boulter, H.J. (1983) *The Philosophy of Charlotte Mason in the 1980s.* London: World-wide Education Service of the PNEU.

Gordon, D. (1981) *100 Great Paintings: Duccio to Picasso.* London: The National Gallery.

Mander, E.K. (undated) *The Gateway to Charlotte Mason — A Tribute to a Great Pioneer.* London: PNEU.

Mason, C. (ed.) (1890–1923) *The Parents' Review.* Journal of the PNEU.

Mason, C. (1896) *Home Education.* London: Kegan Paul, Trench, Trubner.

Mason, C. (1897) *Parents and Children.* London: Kegan Paul, Trench, Trubner.

Mason, C. (1925) *An Essay Towards a Philosophy of Education.* London: J.M. Dent.

WES (1983) *The World-wide Education Service.* Brochure of the World-wide Education Service of the PNEU.

Wilson, R. (1983) *Starting from a Walk.* London: World-wide Education Service of the PNEU.

11

All parents as a resource for education
(Lessons to be drawn from the Sandwell Project)

Carol Stevens

INTRODUCTION

Our present education system, which is over 100 years old, has its roots in the charitable institutions of the late nineteenth century, yet questions concerning its efficiency and efficacy have been the subject of much searching.

In the post-1939–45 era, much emphasis has been placed on the individual child with regard to age, ability and aptitude. This emphasis on the individual child in the school environment implies a necessity for the investigation of other factors outside the child, the most important of these being the family environment. The effect of the family environment on the rate of school progress of many children seems to indicate that the full significance of the environment is not wholly appreciated within our state education system.

> Our educational system, originally moulded by the impress of Victorian economic and social requirements may not yet have been fully adapted to present needs. *(Plowden Report, 1967)*

Plowden furthermore suggests that lack of success is also due to the lack of opportunity for intellectual development existing in many families. Children from a really impoverished background may well have had a normal, satisfactory emotional life. What they often lack is the opportunity to develop intellectual interests. This shows in their poor command of language (Plowden Report, 1967). In the particular part of the West Midlands in which the Sandwell Project was undertaken, there was sufficient evidence from various reports to show deficits in the stimulation and awareness of children at normal school admission age, i.e. nursery 4–reception rising 5. Educational research pointed to the fact that a closer look should be taken at the area and related activities concerning the pre-school period.

> The gap between the educational opportunities of the most and least fortunate children should be closed for economic and social reasons alike. It cannot be done unless extra effort, extra skill, and extra resources are devoted to the task. *(Plowden Report, 1967)*

It was therefore decided to mount an action research in order to assess the quality of 'education' on the basis of our researches into compensatory education aspects (West Bromwich Education Committee, 1970).

> If children are unable to learn, we should assume that we have not, as yet, found the right way to teach them. *(Bullock Report, 1975)*

This was to be the basis for our project, for in this context 'childhood' was an ongoing process and education a concept which took us far beyond the classroom and the school.

PARENTAL INVOLVEMENT IN PRIMARY EDUCATION PROJECT

By 1973 the LEA supported and had obtained financial backing for the 'Parental Involvement in Primary Education Project' which started in 1974. The scheme commenced with four teachers who had the necessary training, experience and motivation.

From the outset the project was considered to be an extension of the Psychology Service's Remedial and Advisory Education Department. Project teachers were based at the Child Guidance Centre and this resulted in possibilities for close liaison and co-operation within the service — an advantage in the search for total family 'treatment'. (Many of the families involved in the project would, by definition, already have been in contact with the service in respect of an older child, or indeed were former pupils who were now parents themselves.) Aimed at the 0–5 age range, the work of the project is seen to have provided a vital downward extension of the existing service.

We shall concentrate on one teacher working in a small industrial area in the north-west of the Metropolitan Borough of Sandwell, formerly the enlarged County Borough of West Bromwich. Four schools were chosen in 1974 from which to select families who might benefit from the project in this one section. (In all, 16 schools were approached initially and now, in 1983, 19 schools are involved.)

Work commenced in only one school, slowly building up to a full visiting load over the first two years. To achieve any real or lasting success it was obvious that there must be a consistency and thoroughness in establishing these first relationships, for they were to form the foundations of change throughout the local community.

All four schools were located near each other, with overlapping catchment areas. Head teachers were in agreement with the proposal after discussions with the Principal Educational Psychologist. Assessment procedure was as follows. The English Picture Vocabulary Test 1 and Pre School Test (Brimer and Dunn, 1962) was used throughout the project, administered to every child up to 5 years 7 months old. Those who failed to achieve a score of 90 were assumed to be experiencing difficulty based on language deprivation. Those who had younger siblings still at home were selected for visiting. Visiting, once established with a family, would continue until their last child was admitted to school. (This means that some families first visited in 1974 are still visited on a weekly basis in 1983 as new siblings appear at regular intervals.)

Proposed action after testing

1. Weekly visits arranged with parent or parents.
2. Visits of 30–45 minutes, depending on age and ability of child or children.
3. Equipment suitable for age and ability to be used during teaching session and left for reinforcement by parents until next visit.
4. Constant stimulation of language and communication within the home and encouragement of confidence in both parent and child.
5. Tactful liaison with other agencies where necessary in order to alleviate associated stresses which might be obstructing normal development.
6. Provision of a link between the home and school in matters where misunderstanding may arise due to poor communication system.

The most important factor is re-education of the family as a whole. Experience suggests that this can be achieved only by the quality and duration of the relationship originally established in the home setting and nurtured through a series of vital phases eventually involving other people and places. It was envisaged that such a visiting programme would cover a prolonged period of time, indicating the development of awareness, both within the family and within the teacher, which might lead the family in a new direction. The long-term aim based on such a relationship was that this personal development and motivation would assist families to maintain self-help initiatives even after official visiting ceased. (Pre-school children *do* eventually reach school age!)

THE EARLY DAYS

All parents experience problems in the process of bringing up their children, whatever their environment or social background. In a declining urban area they are also deeply affected by the economic and physical difficulties that they encounter. Although the selection of families was a standardised procedure and no attempt was made to select on the basis of economic or physical need and deprivation, it was in fact discovered that the majority of those taking part in the scheme were experiencing difficulties in many areas of their lives.

The project is about parents as people and people as parents. They become parents by design, instinct or accident, and much of what they decide to do within their families will be a result of generations of influence, bringing with it the strengths and weaknesses of their culture and background. The urban area abounds with such families already struggling with matters which they consider to be more important than taking an active part in the existing state educational system.

Initially the response of all parents approached was encouraging, regardless of their environment and social disadvantage. Mothers particularly, feeling the consistent support of weekly contact with a caring and supportive visitor, became enlivened and discovered new resources within themselves. By involving themselves in the learning process with their pre-school child they became more understanding and tolerant towards the older children in the family. Subsequent testing of the pre-school child on entry to school showed in most cases a marked improvement over that of the contact child. More tolerant views developing at home also affected the progress of those at school, and teachers noticed improvement in the performance of the contact child even though the PIP (Parental Involvement Project) had not been involved directly with him or her in a teaching situation (although of course he or she is encountered quite often in the family setting when visits are made in holiday periods or evenings). The mother at this stage became very much aware of her role in the appreciation of her children's school interests and more readily questioned them about their day.

In many families the father was at home all day, and he too became part of the educating process, involving himself in the reinforcement of skills and showing more patience and tolerance with an active and questioning child. At this stage school and home attitudes moved more closely together and in some aspects began to coincide. Parents became more aware of the problems faced by a teacher in the classroom and teachers were having to face up to the fact that many of their assumptions about the experiences of their charges were not correct. In many issues previously mishandled, compromise was achieved and the school situation for many children subsequently eased. This was particularly apparent in any negotiations necessary in referral for special schooling for the less able child. This is normally difficult for any family to accept, and was an area of particular concern in my district. Many parents had previously found full co-operation difficult for varying reasons, e.g. their inherent mistrust of authority, feelings of inadequacy and failure, and inability to face up to such a situation generally, where they already felt themselves to be different. Happily, the relationship established between family and the PIP has produced an understanding and a gradual acceptance of handicap which, by close liaison with the remedial and advisory teacher, educational psychologist and school, is effective in achieving full co-operation and a successful placement for the child, in particular with the prospect of a good relationship with school throughout his or her life there.

> A relationship of long standing with parents and a pattern of consistent welcome into their homes proves invaluable when 'bad news' or difficult decisions need to be discussed and acted upon. *(Stevens, 1982)*

The triangle that initially established equality on all three sides — school, home and PIP — does inevitably become distorted as each phase is successfully negotiated. There is often, of necessity, a complete blotting out of the 'school liaison' until it is acceptable to the family, but eventually equilibrium is achieved with the support which is offered. This could never be so if the project were school-based, or indeed institution-based. The goodwill can be made to operate only when generated on the family hearth.

It is apparent that if these families are to succeed in the continual support of their children throughout their school life, teachers must also adapt their views and priorities concerning their expectations of what the children can offer. Adequate consideration should always be given to the pressures and influences which are apparent in the home. Judgements made must always be flexible and easily adapted to avoid labelling a child or a family who has experienced a difficult patch.

A DECADE OF CHANGE, 1974–1983

If we consider the main areas of difficulty experienced by the families involved in the project, a pattern will emerge to indicate that very positive changes in attitude have affected adjustments to the pressures of the present time.

Housing

Housing policy, which left much to be desired at the outset of the project, has changed very little. Some effort has been made to rehouse young families who live in high-rise flats, but it is likely that those who really need it have failed to keep in rent credit and are also on gas/electricity blacklists, thus diminishing their chances of council options. The attitudes generated on both sides by the generally hopeless situation give rise to aggression and inability to communicate, thereby reducing chances of a favourable move. The social stigma of having electricity cut off and being in arrears with rent has, in the past, caused much misery and social isolation for both parents and children. For these families, still in their inadequate dwellings, the improvement here has come in the help they have received from the PIP in adjusting more happily to their circumstances, learning the acceptable approaches to make to the authority concerned and becoming more motivated to accept what they have. Because of the PIP, they are likely to meet others in similar circumstances, and to find the 'social' alternatives they have hitherto felt unable to embrace now more acceptable to them.

Finances

It would appear that financial arrangements are now much more agreeable to the majority of families affected by redundancy and unemployment, e.g. rent and fuel bills deducted at source by the DHSS, leaving them spending money for non-essentials and food. Families who in 1974 were involved in a wave of impulse buying, usually through hire-purchase agreements, now appear to have a less materialistic approach and find that pleasure and involvement are available within their own community. It requires personal efforts which they now feel able to make, but hardly any financial input, thus reinforcing their growing awareness of spiritual, not material, values.

Changing attitudes which at first only directly affected the mother are now involving the father too. Many fathers are at home now and much of the 'foundry–drinking–wife abuse' syndrome has gone, particularly in the under-35 age range, and fathers are playing a much more positive role in the day-to-day upbringing of the children. This does occasionally bring conflict, if parents differ in their ideas on discipline, but even conflict brings conversation, and there is a wider range of language in the average home. Depressed, isolated mothers, who became withdrawn and often neurotic, are now less likely to be alone for such long periods and have a more healthy outlet for their feelings in direct and instant discussions. The alternative to this was the total repression of such feelings and vague threats of what would happen when Dad came home. The tensions in such families are very much alleviated now by their enforced proximity. It would appear that other tensions, due to the proximity, have a less damaging effect on the children and their language development. The child now has access to an extended family more often, as enforced leisure gives greater opportunity for family visits and outings.

Attitudes to health

Fathers who are at home are more likely to become agitated by symptoms, and there appears to be much abuse of the medical services by over-protective fathers who insist on instant medical treatment for something the mother might have put off, or coped with. They panic much more readily and will involve themselves immediately in the machinery of doctor–hospital–chemist. It would appear that when they were spending their time in the male world, i.e. working and drinking, all this was left to the discretion of the wife, who rarely took such action. In many cases it was a question of 'What the eye can't see, the heart doesn't grieve over'. This applies also to the standards of hygiene in the home. There has been a very real improvement in housekeeping and cleanliness, again initiated (if not performed) by the father.

'Linguistic deprivation is the commonest and intellectually most damaging of all.' Short goes on to say that 'Whatever educational provision we make, mother is the young child's principal teacher'. Very often she is untrained and ill-equipped for such tasks as teaching her child his or her native language (Short, 1974).

My experience has been that in many homes the day-to-day stresses, poor health and all other manifestations of 'ill-being' as opposed to 'well-being' mean that education in any form is bottom of the list of priorities, and that achieving an awareness in the parents of the need for their active involvement in an education programme cannot be done in a short time.

It is often impossible for the PIP to change the physical disadvantages besetting a family or indeed the lifestyle adopted by that family. The aim has never been to do this by implication or interference. What is attempted is the support of a young mother so that she grows up emotionally and has a sounding board for her ideas, opinions and values. These will always be there below the aggressive defence mechanisms, the obscene outbursts against officialdom, the inertia, the resignation and the depression. Too easily acquired Valium is not the answer.

My visit is often a 'space' in which the mother can express herself, possibly for the first time since her schooldays, to another person whose reaction will not be discouraging or authoritarian. The way in which she views her domestic situation and measures her own worth as a human being will gradually change. The outcome is that she will look outside herself and her own situation, see others who are worse off and find a potential within herself to give. When this point is reached for these reasons and through the slow evaluation of self, practical difficulties assume less importance and attitudes to home, family and the social system become more tolerant.

The mother and/or father are then ready to offer others in the community help towards the same goal. This is neither planned nor even acknowledged, but results from the see-saw of the need to take and the need to give on which I first embarked with them. They now sit at the giving end, and the opportunity for action is always there. Specific problems experienced by families, e.g. husbands or elder sons serving prison sentences, frequent hospitalisation of children, very anti-social neighbours, are a common bond unexperienced by PIP, so help of varying kinds offered by individuals in the community is likely to be more fruitful than professional counselling.

THE NEXT STEP: PARENTS AS TEACHERS, BUT NOT IN SCHOOL

In fulfilling these needs we have developed, in the latter part of the project, twice-weekly meetings in 'another place'. The other place is a building. This involves daytime use at certain specified times during the week in term time and throughout the long summer holiday when schools are closed. It provides a very worthwhile extension for many of our families. It is geographically central to four out of five of the schools involved and has no direct connection with any of them, the common denominator being myself and all the families taking part in the project. It is, therefore, ideal for our purposes, giving mothers a rare opportunity for mixing in a multi-school group and enabling them, because of their personal link with me, to overcome the usual frictions inherent in such a gathering. In this place counselling, advice, practical help, friendship, education (and a great degree of joy) are available, offered willingly by all those who are able, to all those who have yet to travel further. Personal achievement in the group has been rapid. The reliability and degree of responsibility taken by the non-professionals can often put me and my colleagues to shame. The resulting sense of fellowship and belonging produces an atmosphere which would have been impossible to establish if the initiation of the scheme had involved committee decisions, a purpose-built site, and planned expert and professional staffing.

The summer holiday activities are geared to providing education and leisure within the normal environment of the children and families, with great personal input by the community itself. Attendance varies be- tween 70 and 100 people. All children must be accompanied by a parent or an adult relative, enabling families (not necessarily involved in the same activity) to enjoy their leisure together in a constructive and enriching way. 'Our other place' provides the second stage in a self-help process. Born leaders emerge, and parents are able to offer special skills confidently without fear of rejection or failure. The new, shy, wary people who are just starting the process know that no-one here will ridicule them or their tentative efforts to help. Expectations are low; there is tolerance and genuine understanding in abundance.

In 1982 we were able to provide a seaside holiday for three of our families (separately); the mothers involved had all given a tremendous amount of their time and energy to the successful running of 'our other place'. All three experienced hardships and difficulties themselves without grumbling or expecting anything. Two of those concerned had indeed been extremely withdrawn and shy and had been operating far below their social potential when I first knew them. One of the outcomes of the holiday, which was financed by a sponsored marathon run by two of our remedial and advisory teachers, was a letter received quite unexpectedly by one of the runners. At no time had I suggested that a thank-you of this type was necessary. It will be obvious that the use of language in this letter and the presentation indicate a great unrealised potential, constantly frustrated by social and financial bur- dens. Here are some extracts from the letter.

It was a gorgeous week, full of the little things so important to a growing family.

We were thrilled by the beautiful countryside — excited at the sight of the sea and beguiled by the girls' reaction to everything they saw. For myself, I had a carefree week without the normal day to day worries. Even my husband (on whose behalf I thank you too) had a unique opportunity to take leadership and daily led us over mountain trails, down streams, and through pastures. You not only gave us a holiday break and a new outlook on life, but a week loaded with memories to last us a lifetime.

May I add the PS:

On the 'wet days' — I'm afraid numerous — the girls collected slates, cones, lichens and other natural oddments and with the purchase of one tube of adhesive, created small sculptures and stone ornaments, which were brought back as gifts instead of the normal seaside memorabilia — Mine still has pride of place!

CONCLUSION

Fitting into the system

Experience has led us to agree with the late Mia Kellmer Pringle, who said in 1975:

That as the foundations in a house are much more important to put right than if something is wrong with the roof, so the foundations for later behaviour, for relations with other people and for how we get on with ourselves, are laid down during the earlier months and years. These months are vital to later life. *(Kellmer Pringle, 1975)*

For many of the young parents involved in the project the foundations were unsound and they battled along in the conventional systems unsuitably armed with the acceptable communication skills necessary to achieve an easier passage for themselves and their children.

The aims of the project were never to offer these families an alternative educational system but an alternative educational facility to enable them to have continued access to the present system and the experience and personal ability to cope with all its restraints and conformities. That many of them failed themselves, particularly in the secondary stages of their own school life, is an important factor when working towards this aim. To encourage them to seek an alternative school system would be totally wrong, in my opinion, because their new area of success and personal achievement must be in exactly the same field as their previous failure. They must learn to take their rightful place in the existing society which at some time, however far back, rejected them. Even if ill-equipped materially, families who have benefited most from the Sandwell Project are the ones who have clung to their culture, developed the strengths that it offered, wisely abandoned its weaknesses, and found themselves able to operate confidently alongside others who, it would appear, have suffered less disadvantage.

Milestones towards confidence

1. Many find they have a more optimistic outlook and will readily cheer up others who have lost hope.
2. Original contact children, now in comprehensive school, find that their parents are able to initiate, establish and maintain a good and productive pastoral relationship with the school on their behalf.
3. Aggressive confrontations with various authorities make way for reasonable discussion and debate in achieving a solution acceptable to both parties.
4. Parents regain their sense of humour about themselves and the world around them, hitherto completely smothered by the apparent hopelessness of their physical and social situation.
5. They now appear to be adults with choices and acceptance patterns of behaviour at their fingertips to help in the decision-making involved in such choices.
6. Alongside the confidence and personal growth comes organisation of their daily life and a more positive and balanced approach to events by which the family are affected, and a more knowledgeable understanding of personal relationships inside and outside the home.

The future

In the project, education seems to have come full circle, from child to parent and back again to child. The learning process has indeed been taken beyond the school and into the streets. Evidence shows already that families who have long since ceased to be actively part of the project continue to direct their lives in a more enlightened way and continue to maintain all the improvements and progress first noted, in spite of the fact that weekly support is completely withdrawn.

It appears that this is education for life, for living with one's fellow human beings, for giving all the opportunity to serve and offer skills, however small, with confidence and dignity. What they have learned, they will never lose. Actions they have grown courageous enough to take, they will take again (it is easier the second time). They will take control of their own future. Subsequent families will benefit and, it is envisaged, will fit far more readily into their generation whatever its particular expectation of them. For what we have all discovered together, while working alongside each other, is that the potential for this kind of success lies within all human beings, deprived and privileged alike, and knows no limits of fashion, trend or time.

REFERENCES

Brimer, M. and Dunn, L. (1962) *English Picture Vocabulary Test.* Newnham: Educational Evaluation Enterprises.

Bullock Report (1975) *A Language for Life.* Report of the Committee of Enquiry App. Secretary of State for Education and Science under Chairmanship of Sir Alan Bullock FBA. London: HMSO.

Kellmer Pringle, M.L. (1975) Young children need full time mother, *Listener,* 10 October.

Plowden Report (1967) *Children and their Primary Schools.* A report of the Central Advisory Council for Education, Volume 1. London: HMSO.

Short, E. (1974) *Birth to 5.* London: HMSO.

Stevens, C. (1982) Parental involvement, in Hinson, M. and Hughes, M. *Planning Effective Progress.* Amersham: Hulton-NARE.

West Bromwich Education Committee (1970) *Teacher Guide to Compensatory Education.*

12

Flexischooling

Roland Meighan

INTRODUCTION

Jennifer, aged 13 and writing in 1969, produces what seems to be a foolish idea: 'Perhaps in the not too distant future, man's intelligence will have improved so much that children will be able to be taught by their parents in the home' (Blishen, 1969). Events rather than people's intelligence appear to be catching up with Jennifer's speculation. These events include the expansion of information systems like CEEFAX, ORACLE and PRESTEL, the collapse of work with the advent of micro-processors, and educational innovations like the Open University, Flexistudy and Education Otherwise.

At the same time, disillusionment with contemporary schooling continues. One outcome is the growth of home-based schooling in the UK, the USA and elsewhere. Most families take this course of action out of desperation, a few in an attempt to develop an alternative lifestyle and a few as a calculated, deliberate action, suspecting that school may be doing their children as much harm as good. This last group contains many teachers who are also parents and who, with the insight of insiders, want to do better for their own children. Hemming (1980) puts their feelings bluntly, for he entitles his book evaluating the secondary schooling system in the UK *The Betrayal of Youth*. He pleads for radical changes in the approaches adopted. His analysis is psychological, emphasising the brain functions overstressed and those suppressed by contemporary secondary schooling. Another analysis is sociological, emphasising the influence of the hidden curriculum of schooling in suppressing diversity, resulting in inflexible, dogmatic, intolerant and authoritarian people in rather large numbers (Meighan, 1981a). The main ideas of this analysis are contained in this satirical passage:

> The children mounted a series of tableaux demonstrating how they are preparing for Real Life. First there was a demonstration of playground brawling, with obvious analogies with the sort of fisticuffs to be expected during any adult's normal working week. Then there was bullying, name-calling, racial abuse, and intimidation, all vital in learning how to behave rationally in the future.
>   Next Mr Alcock showed how school life, with its emphasis on mindless repetition, routine, excruciating boredom, senseless uniformity, internecine competition, prison clothing, regimentation, and the crushing of originality, was precisely the preparation necessary for the future, in which most people will work in extremely large organisations doing repetitive mindless tasks, and living their lives with the sole ambition of achieving a higher position in the pecking order. It all led up to a splendid finale in which the whole school trooped on in perfect drill, wearing faceless masks, and engaged in a general melee representing Progress.
> *(Education Otherwise, 1981)*

Schooling does not *have* to be like this, and many attempts exist to avoid the worst of the above features, as Hemming points out and as case studies like those of Watts (1977 and 1980) indicate. One pupil reflects on her schooling in the account of Watts (1980):

> Compulsion seems like a kind of madness, an insanity when I think of Countesthorpe and its room for flexibility and freedom.

Schooling has more educational potential, Watts argues, if it becomes open and flexible. Harber takes up similar issues in Chapter 4 of this book.

FLEXISCHOOLING

There are many alternatives on offer as the solution to the problems of education. Authoritarian people seeking the illusion of certainty advocate well tried but outdated systems like public schools, grammar schools and comprehensive schools. Their non-authoritarian critics, knowing the evidence that denotes these systems to be inadequate, provide support for other ideas: deschooling, state-supported democratic schools, 'little' schools on the Danish model, schools within schools or education at home. Sometimes these are seen as an alternative orthodoxy, sometimes as part of a diversity of provisions. Russell (1932) was keen to point out the dangers of exchanging orthodoxies:

Orthodoxy is the grave of intelligence, no matter what orthodoxy it may be. And in this respect, the orthodoxy of the radical is no better than that of the reactionary.

One approach that would tolerate considerable diversity and avoid the problems of replacing one orthodoxy with another is that of flexischooling.

Flexischooling can be seen as an amalgam of ideas obtained from the practices of the Open University and flexistudy systems in further education, adult education and correspondence colleges. An extract from the *Flexistudy* manual of Barnet College (1978) gives the bare bones of the approach:

Flexistudy combines the flexibility of correspondence courses with face-to-face contact and other advantages of day or evening classes.

Flexistudy students study at home, at their own pace and at times to suit themselves, using the highly successful study packs issued by the National Extension College, Cambridge. In addition, they come to Barnet College from time to time to meet the tutors who have been marking their written work and also meet other students following the same courses.

These Flexistudy tutorial meetings are fixed by mutual arrangement at the times and on the days convenient to students. For instance, they might only be held monthly, perhaps on a Tuesday evening one month, a Saturday morning the next and so on. Or whatever suits students and tutor.

So if you cannot come to a fixed class evey week, if you are, say, on shift-work, the head of a one-parent family, someone who gets home too late from factory or office or often has to work out of town, or if you just don't want to tie yourself down to time and place, contact Barnet College about Flexistudy.

There are nearly 30 subjects to choose from, ranging from Basic Maths to Sociology 'A' level, from French for Beginners to 'A' level Biology or just simply How to Study Effectively.

In making such an approach available as a flexischooling system, a variety of arrangements are possible. 'Contracts' between parents and school could be based on 100 per cent, 75 per cent, 50 per cent, 25 per cent or almost no time in school according to home circumstances at a particular time. The administrative problems seem immense: however, the Open University copes with 30 000 students, all on individual schedules, while correspondence colleges cope effectively with monitoring their students' study programmes. One full-time evening institute organiser may have 25 000 students on twelve different sites with a variety of part-time teachers. In other words, the administrative know-how to cope with complex flexible arrangements already exists.

Flexischooling can be seen to be based on rather different assumptions from those of current schooling:

1. There does not have to be a single location for education. There can be several, including homes and school buildings in particular but also museums, libraries, parks and workplaces. The position of school as the sole location for education has only recently been questioned (Meighan and Brown, 1980).
2. Home resources can be utilised in educational programmes, e.g. television, radio, cassette recorders and the postal service.
3. Parents can be seen as part of the solution of the problems of education rather than as part of the problem and can learn or even be trained to have an active role in co-operative programmes with schools (Meighan, 1981b). The World-wide Education Service has been training parents by correspondence to educate their children for over 100 years, as Boulter points out in Chapter 10.
4. Learners can learn a great deal without a teacher being present. Correspondence colleges have always appreciated this point, as does the World-wide Education Service with its experience in helping expatriate families to educate their children in foreign countries or in the UK. The concept of distance learning has developed credibility in the work of the Open University.

If some of these ideas bring to mind the notion of deschooling, this should cause no surprise. The group of writers rather misleadingly known as the deschoolers were, for the most part, in favour of regenerating schooling in various ways. The central concept in their analysis was that of the hidden curriculum which stressed uncritical conformity and suppressed diversity. This concept has been developed and extended considerably in the ten years since these writers produced their books (Meighan, 1981a). But it is the changes in technology and the consequent collapse of work that are forcing a reconsideration of the idea of regenerating schooling. A recent Manifesto for Change was signed by leading figures (e.g. Lord Butler, former Minister of Education, and Edward Carpenter, Dean of Westminster) from all sectors of British society and published in *The Times Educational Supplement* in January 1981. It stressed the idea that schools as currently organised were incapable of producing the flexible people needed to cope with a rapidly changing society, the decline of work and the increase in leisure.

CHANGES IN THE TECHNICAL AND ECONOMIC CONTEXTS

The role of public education is now challenged by a number of changes in technology and the application of these in economic contexts, so that conventional occupational structures are in a process of metamorphosis popularly referred to as the 'collapse of work' (Jenkins and Sherman, 1979).

The influence of the now familiar technology of communications such as television and radio has until now largely rivalled that of schools. Homes are well equipped with television and radio — over 90 per cent of households have these facilities, according to consumer surveys — and in this respect most classrooms are museum pieces by comparison. The messages carried show marked contrasts. Textbooks containing dated information and ideas, interpreted by teachers whose stock of knowledge was obtained several years ago, compete with a science programme like BBC's *Tomorrow's World* and with well researched and presented documentaries on social and political affairs. The response of the educational establishment has often been akin to that of King Canute: to ignore the tide that is coming in or indeed, order it to go away. The pretence is that as a cultural carrier the mass media are complementary rather than competitive. But, to change the historical analogy, the schooling cavalry, equipped with sword, is about to face the heavy artillery if not the guided missiles. Recent trends are tilting the odds in favour of home-based education (Meighan and Reid, 1982).

It is no longer necessary to speculate about the new information systems. They are already here. The marketing drives that established first radio, then black and white television and finally colour television are now turning to the information systems of CEEFAX, ORACLE and ORBIT. The GPO has its own system, PRESTEL, and it already has a long waiting list for installations. Simultaneously the marketing of video recorders for domestic use is taking place. Personal computers costing around £100 that plug into television receivers are also aimed at the domestic market. In quite a short time, five to ten years perhaps, the majority of homes are likely to be equipped with even more sophisticated information retrieval centres than they are at present, while schools, starved of the necessary funds, will be able to do little more than replace old textbooks. All these changes in communication and information systems are taking place in the context of what is popularly known as the knowledge explosion: it is estimated that knowledge is doubling in quantity every ten years. Much of this new knowledge renders existing ideas and information out of date, incomplete or inaccurate, and access to the sources of updating is increasing in homes more than schools. The pretence that these information sources are complementing rather than competing with the school as a carrier of culture is becoming difficult to sustain.

The metamorphosis of conventional occupational structures is taking place alongside these changes in communication and information systems. Jenkins and Sherman (1979) demonstrate that the trend towards large-scale unemployment in the Western European nations had begun before the advent of the micro-processor technology; the latter has escalated the trend rather than caused it. The key characteristics of micro-processor based computers is that they are cheap, portable and durable. Computing tasks that could be done only on computers in special buildings and costing thousands of pounds can now be done on a small machine the size of a large office typewriter costing £500 or so. Factories and offices can be run with tens of people rather than hundreds or thousands. It is the view of these two writers that the top priority for education is the preparation for leisure. This concern is already a key concern in homes, for high on the agenda is the use of evenings, weekends and holidays. In some cases work is coming back to homes as a result of micro-processors. In the UK, ICL has about 60 programmers who have their computer terminals at home. In the USA, banking concerns are beginning to locate word processors in the homes so that workers can do company work at home.

However, the current fashion in education is to cling to myths about school as a preparation for work, and 'work' is largely defined as 'the manufacturing sector of the economy'. Curiously, this is already only a small sector of the economy containing less than 7 million people out of an adult population of about 41 million. It is estimated that this figure could halve in the next decade, not least because of robotisation in manufacturing industry, and the growing unemployment figures suggest that this is already happening quite rapidly. The figure of 15 million adults who do not work because they are retired, running households or unemployed is expected to increase considerably as a result. The remaining 26 million who work in central and local government, the professions, the retail industry, transport and the entertainment and leisure industries are also subject to the collapse of work. Jenkins and Sherman note how each of these sectors is affected by the advent of micro-processor technology. In such circumstances, stressing the top priority of schools as preparation for work seems very short-sighted, if not ridiculous.

EDUCATIONAL DEVELOPMENTS

Several recent educational developments have involved homes in a systematic way as both a base and a learning resource. The most dramatic in terms of scale has been that of the Open University. Here the major base for learning is the home, supplemented by occasional study centre meetings and summer schools of a week's duration. The resources of the home are absorbed into the network of learning experiences, in particular special programmes on radio and television, but also the telephone, the tape recorder, and even the kitchen as a home laboratory for science experiments. The postal service operates as a major means of communication. Moreover, some of the learning experiences, such as viewing a TV programme, can be shared with other members of the family. Many new Open University students have been recruited by 'catching' the interest of an existing student member of the family.

A less dramatic idea, though of no less significance, has been the concept of flexistudy as developed in a number of colleges of further education. Flexistudy provides for the home to be used as the main base for study, the college being used as a resource during regular visits. Here students can meet tutors, use the library or make use of any other college facilities that they need at a particular time.

The use of parents in a teaching role is a further development. The most marked examples have been those parents who have elected to educate their children at home. In the UK the organisation Education Otherwise is a mutual aid venture undertaken by such parents. In the USA there is a similar organisation called Growing Without Schooling. Sadly, the polarised situation of *either* home *or* school has been forced on such parents by the unimaginative response of many LEA officials. The idea of a co-operative programme, a flexistudy arrangement, or some other home-school partnership which is the first choice of many families who turn to home-based education, has not materialised yet, though it is probably only a matter of time before the chief education officer of some LEA sees the advantages of such schemes, and indeed in the USA this has already happened in some states, as Holt (1981) notes.

IN LOCO PARENTIS

In organising schools, much play has been made of the idea of teachers taking on the responsibilities that would otherwise be the parents', e.g. supervision, control and pastoral care. However, as parents differ in their interpretation of these matters, the position of inflexible schools is difficult. Many schools have corporal punishment, and in this have the support of some parents. Other parents who do not physically punish their children at home refuse the right of teachers to do so at school, and the recent European Court of Human Rights judgement upholds both their right to this refusal and their entitlement to damages if the right is abused.

In a discussion of the practicalities of flexischooling, one head teacher saw this as a means of resolving some of his difficulties. If a unit of his school were staffed by those teachers on his staff who were sympathetic to the idea of parents with different ideas of control, education and the role of parents as educators, contracts between these parents and the school units could be agreed and implemented without infringing the rights of those parents who wanted a different regime and total attendance at school. Such a unit would redefine some of the problems of truants and pupils reacting against formal school regimes as variations rather than rejection. As part of a flexischooling provision, contracts involving parents, pupils and teachers could, in effect, make agreed truancy for education reasons legitimate, and educational social workers could reserve their energies for other tasks.

This head teacher had reached the same conclusion as Watts (1980). Watts gives an account of the 'sub-school solution' where units within a school have a high degree of autonomy so that pupils, teachers and parents work to an agreed 'covenant'. He goes on to offer a draft covenant for pupils, teachers and parents of some three pages in length.

Interestingly, this approach might well work for the parent-teacher democratic small schools of the Campaign for State-Supported Alternative Schools outlined in Chapter 8 by Laura Diamond. Whether this was incorporated into a flexischooling unit or operated as a separate unit would depend on circumstances.

There are strong links here with the idea of Schools Within Schools in the USA and with the ideas of Barth (1980) in *Run School, Run,* where diversity in regimes is encouraged and tolerated as an alternative to the notion of a regimentalised school operating to some notion of a 'one right way'. Flexischooling adds to these ideas the notion of location variation: some of the learning can be done at home with those parents who wish to take on a more active role in the education of their children. The capability of parents to do this is now more a matter of fact than of speculation (see Meighan, 1981b).

Flexischooling might even help cope with the difficult problems created by multicultural situations. The demand for separate Moslim schools because of clashes over parts of the curriculum such as PE for girls and RE teaching and for mother-tongue teaching might be accommodated in a flexischooling unit.

FLEXISCHOOLING, IDEOLOGIES OF EDUCATION AND THE TEACHER'S ROLE

Earlier in this chapter reference was made to the changed assumptions underpinning flexischooling as compared with certain features of contemporary schooling. Some of the ideas are linked with the ideas of the 'deschooling' writers. This raises the question of whether flexischooling is one of the competing ideologies of education. Now an ideology of education, as I have argued elsewhere (Meighan, 1981a), is made up of several component entities or 'theories':

(a) a theory of knowledge, its content and structure;
(b) a theory of learning and the learner's role;
(c) a theory of teaching and the teacher's role;
(d) a theory of resources appropriate for learning;
(e) a theory of assessment of whether learning has been successful;
(f) a theory of organisation of learning situations;
(g) a theory of aims, objectives or outcomes;
(h) a theory of language and its usage.

It is clear that flexischooling has something to say about more than one of these, but since it does not have something to say about all of them, it does not, of itself, constitute an ideology of education, and it can therefore serve several existing or alternative ideologies. Flexischooling is ideologically flexible, for it could serve a traditional view of knowledge and assessment as the Open University has done, or it could serve an autonomous ideology of education stressing self-directed learning, or any other view of education. It is more accurately seen as an alternative method of educating, though one that challenges some of the assumptions about existing methods, including their cost, for if schools increasingly limit themselves to doing those things you cannot do at home or elsewhere, costs must go down. Flexischooling holds out the possibility of being an administrator's dream: a method that both is cheaper and yields better results.

Flexischooling also holds out the possibility of a changed role for school teachers and makes their task more like that of their high-status cousins, university teachers. This role requires a wide range of skills for tutorial, instructional, consultancy and research tasks. Both the interest and the demands of this role are indicated in this passage from the Barnet College *Flexistudy* manual:

(a) Involve carefully-structured course material with appropriate references to published works.

(b) Involve, if necessary, preliminary work on study skills.
(c) Utilise all the available college resources.
(d) Provide sufficient opportunities for feedback to the tutor through the post, telephone and personal contact.
(e) Allow for the bringing-together of students following the same course in face-to-face discussions with other students on the same course.
(f) Enable the students to get the best possible advice in the shortest possible time.
(g) Be sufficiently flexible to incorporate developments in Tele-text and view-data systems which would enable the communication to take place not only between the College and the students but use external referral agencies.

In short we wanted to devise a system that would provide a total resource package centred on the individual part-time student — written materials, face-to-face tuition, audio-visual aids, access to library facilities, career guidance, social contact and general advice — where the student could have easy access to any particular resources as and when required.

CONCLUSIONS

If we accept the verdict of Hemming and others that the outcome of much of the contemporary secondary schooling system constitutes a 'betrayal of youth', then the onus is upon us to devise something better. Hemming stresses that he is aware that many schools try very hard: it is not effort that is necessarily in question, but the basic design of schooling and the outdated assumptions on which it is based. Hemming has his own ideas about the regeneration of schooling, as have the members of groups advocating state-supported democratic schools or education at home, or schools within schools. It is the proposition of this paper that flexischooling is an approach that could be implemented in a considerable variety of forms, not replacing schools but as part of a diversification of provision and contributing to a regenerated system suitable for the complex and changing needs of a modern, pluralistic democracy.

REFERENCES

Barnet College (1978) *Flexistudy*. Barnet College.

Barth, R. (1980) *Run School, Run*. London: Harvard University Press.

Blishen, E. (1969) *The School That I'd Like*. Harmondsworth: Penguin.

Education Otherwise Newsletter No. 19, September 1981, p. 69.

Hemming, J. (1980) *The Betrayal of Youth*. London: Marion Boyars.

Holt, J. (1981) *Teach Your Own*. London: Lighthouse Books.

Jenkins, C. and Sherman, B. (1979) *The Collapse of Work*. London: Eyre Methuen.

Meighan, R. (1981a) *A Sociology of Educating*. Eastbourne: Holt, Rinehart and Winston.

Meighan, R. (1981b) A new teaching force? Some issues by seeing parents as educators and the implications for teacher education, *Educational Review*, **33** (2).

Meighan, R. and Brown, C. (1980) Locations of learning and ideologies of education, in Barton, L., Meighan, R. and Walker, S. (ed.) *Schooling, Ideology and the Curriculum*. Lewes: Falmer Press.

Meighan, R. and Reid, W. (1982) How will the new technology change the curriculum? *Journal of Curriculum Studies*, **14** (4).

Russell, B. (1932) *Education and the Social Order*. London: George Allen & Unwin.

Times Educational Supplement (1981) Manifesto for Change, 30 January.

Watts, J. (1977) *The Countesthorpe Experience*. London: George Allen & Unwin.

Watts, J. (1980) *Towards an Open School*. Harlow: Longman.

13

Technology, educational technology, independent learning and autonomy

Mary Geffen

INTRODUCTION

If you believe that society has already moved into a phase of technological revolution, as I do, then you are bound to believe that the curriculum of schools must change radically. But certain characteristics of teaching are remarkably persistent. Does this story sound familiar? In my junior school in the 1930s it was a reward for a good pupil daily to colour in a small sun or cloud into a square of a weather chart. Although I studied geography for a further twelve years, this was the nearest I ever got to measuring the climate. In the playground of that school was a little square railing and, inside it, a rusty, shallow cylinder on a plinth. We thought it might be a grave or a memorial: almost right, for I later realised it must have been for measuring rainfall — a monument to the educational philosophy of some long gone late Victorian. Later I proved to be good at converting the silhouette of an imaginary landscape into a map, filling in the contour lines with fine black ink and getting an impressive finish with water-colour wash. My reward was happily bashing a wet mass of torn newspaper and glue into a model mountain with contours 'for the slow ones to copy'. This was a corrupted version of 'learning by doing', I later realised: 'doing' became a reward for being able to symbolise rather than a route towards the understanding of abstractions.

One need not go back to the 1930s to find vestiges of some progressivist episode that has lost its way, and now in the 1980s, with a generation of more and less successful curriculum innovations behind us, we know that the school curriculum is not merely the outcome of putting the best educational theories, know-how and tools (i.e. technologies) into practice. It is a much more complex amalgam of the expectations of professional institutions, examining bodies, industries, parents, government and even children. And all this is contained within an existing stock of books, buildings, teachers and teacher-educators. Perhaps the 'cultural archetype' (Thelen, 1981) represented by schools and classrooms themselves is an even more powerful barrier to change; the conscript student and the employee teacher are both controlled by notions of 'proper behaviour' during the process of schooling.

It is not cynicism, therefore, but a realistic assumption that although by 1990 the current revolution in micro-technology will be creating massive social changes requiring radical educational responses, the effect on the school curriculum will be minimal. We shall see superficial changes: one micro-computer in every classroom and children capable of getting results out of the programs provided for them — a saleable skill. But the robust cultural archetype of schooling will stand between teachers and their capacity to produce a generation of citizens who see information technology as a force that they can handle. Instead, for most future citizens, the computer will be a black box that impinges on their everyday lives primarily as power in the service of the powerful. Unless . . .

EDUCATION AND TECHNOLOGY

In this chapter I shall .explore some of the kinds of educational technology that are available to the independent learner in and out of school in the general context of the other technological changes which are already affecting society at large. By educational technology I do not mean (as people often do) merely the use of audio-visual aids. I mean that anyone who sets out to teach something arranges an environment in which they intend learners to do things — maybe a classroom, a computer, a book, a television programme, or a set of packaged materials. 'Teaching' nowadays includes skills such as graphic design, authorship and computer programming, as well as skills of designing lessons and handling classrooms. The term 'educational technology' takes in this total environment and its wide range of pedagogical skills.

Through these technologies, and especially through media of mass communication, people currently learn and re-learn beyond their school lives. They use, for example, BBC education programmes, home computers, video replay, libraries, language cassettes, and a wide range of periodicals that teach everything from photography to pigeon breeding. Knowledge has for the moment escaped from buildings paid for by educational authorities, and access to knowledge is increasingly a matter of money and new know-how: control of this access to knowledge is shifting to those who are skilful or powerful with the technologies, and a new class barrier is growing between the information-rich and the information-poor.

Such a gap has always existed, but it mattered less when the bulk of our population could depend on work for their sense of purpose, for dignity and for an income. This work ethic persists, but technological unemployment is becoming a way of life for substantial populations. Fifty years ago Keynes wrote:

> The strenuous purposeful money-makers may carry all of us along with them into the lap of economic abundance. But it will be those peoples who can keep alive, and cultivate into a fuller perfection, the art of life itself and do not sell themselves for the means of life, who will be able to enjoy the abundance when it comes.
>
> Yet there is no country and no people, I think, who can look forward to the age of leisure and of abundance without a dread. It is a fearful problem for the ordinary person, with no special talents, to occupy himself, especially if he no longer has roots in the soil or in custom or in the beloved conventions of a traditional society . . .
>
> When the accumulation of wealth is no longer of high social importance, there will be great changes in the code of morals. We shall be able to rid ourselves of many of the pseudo-moral principles which have hag-ridden us for two hundred years, by which we have exalted some of the most distasteful of human qualities into the position of the highest virtues. We shall be able to afford to dare to assess the money-motive at its true value. *(Jones, 1982)*

This change is now upon us. To make it we shall need citizens who are capable of using the resources around them either to create their own work (if they need it) or to make their own lives rich, eventful and meaningful.

EDUCATIONAL TECHNOLOGY AND INDEPENDENT LEARNING

In educational terms, future society needs citizens who are self-directed, not 'other-directed' or 'inner-directed' (after Riesmann, 1951), and who have the skill of recognising what they need to know and the capacity to find out how to learn it. My own view is that such learners need and will use a wide variety of different learning strategies. They will need to be independent learners in the fullest sense. Given the relatively inert superstructure of schooling, certification and socialisation which we have now, and which we seem set to perpetuate in the current schemes for training youth for the sorts of jobs that will not reappear, what contribution can educational technology make?

There are four possibilities: first, educational materials that relieve teachers in classrooms of some of their tasks and free them for others; second, educational materials intended to be used 'at a distance', i.e. distance packages for 'independent' students; and third, students who devise their own learning 'independently', choosing their own learning materials 'off the peg'. It is already obvious that the word 'independent' needs to be used carefully. In these three cases, students could in reality have little independence. On the contrary, they may be extremely dependent, constrained in what they learn and how they learn by the designers of the materials they use. There is therefore a fourth case: those more independent learners who, whatever the content and materials they choose, adopt their own learning styles rather than the style of the teacher or of the material's designer. I shall look at these four cases in turn, with the underlying assumption that our future society needs citizens capable of learning and re-learning truly independently, i.e. autonomously, with complete freedom of choice and access. These ideal learners would have the capacity to identify and formulate their purpose in studying and an awareness of the whole range of materials, especially alternatives suitable for them; they would be able to recognise and use a wide range of learning styles at will; they would have access and power to select and acquire what they want, access to counselling during the process of choice, and the power to withdraw if they chose. This specification is rather like the economist's definition of the perfect buyer in the perfect market who exists only as a figment of a theoretical argument. It is useful for putting a case.

In general, teaching tools or teaching materials are designed to replace some of the teacher's functions. They have been organised and processed according to some theory of what their users should learn and some model of the way they should learn it. This model is frequently implicit. Compare, for example, a sand tray with a sandy beach, or a nature trail with nature.

Whereas in classroom teaching, teachers tend to plan mentally, sometimes leaving quite important options open right up to the moment of action (Clark and Yinger, 1979), teaching tools are complete products, the act of teaching having become frozen into the materials. Many of the concepts applicable to industrial design or to architecture can also be applied to teaching tools: for instance, it is becoming clear that, just like the users of street furniture, students will try to adapt products to their own learning purposes irrespective of the designer's purpose. And designers will react either by making their product 'user-proof' or by aiming it deliberately at a range of optional flexible uses. Further, just as a user of a manufactured product may prefer wood to plastic or wool to silk, similarly the characteristics of the media used for teaching materials are more or less congenial to learners and have an influence analogous to that of the hidden curriculum of the classroom. The appearance of a table of figures and the choice of an image (or, in the world of computer-assisted learning, the 'user-friendliness' of software) become factors that affect learning experiences. Teachers of the future will therefore need the capacity to analyse and evaluate media and the skill to recognise whatever image of the learning process has been designed into the materials, for example whether they extend or restrict learners' choices. But for good or ill, the packaging of educational material will grow, and I believe that it *ought* to grow. Media such as print, tape, video disc and film all have liberating teaching potential and, to say the least, unless they are used more, the cultural gulf between what children do during their formal education and what they do with the rest of their lives will become even larger than it is now.

To what extent is this optimism justified in the first of my four cases, teaching tools in classrooms? In a recent large-scale study of classroom teaching, Maurice Galton and his colleagues (Galton, Simon and Croll, 1980) report that 'independent' learners, i.e. children working alone at tasks and work cards, were commonplace, but the Plowden principle, they remark, is far from being implemented; problem-solving in co-operative groups is rare. On the other hand, Ian Westbury (Westbury, 1973) argues that if primary classroom teaching is to become more open, teachers must be released for facilitative helping roles and their other teaching functions shifted onto artifacts. He cites Dienes rods and learning toys that children pick up incidentally around the classroom and argues that similar design principles could be extended using technologies such as advertising and television. The essence of these teaching tools is that they create the kind of interaction that a single child may have with a good teacher. I have summarised the characteristics he requires of them below:

1. They must enable students to identify their own learning task.
2. The activity they provoke must be intrinsically rewarding, self-pacing, sustaining and engaging.
3. They must generate understanding and mastery; the central principles of the subject matter must either be designed into the materials or be inherent (e.g. as in sand play).
4. They must bridge from existing experiences to new knowledge; the natural environment is sometimes inadequate as a basis for learning

and then simulated experiences must be contrived and embodied in teaching tools.

5. They must be self-instructing and self-managing, producing feedback which enables children to learn from their experience.
6. They must enable the averagely keen teacher to cope with mixed simultaneous learning activities.
7. They must provoke question-asking and keep learners active.
8. They must involve the whole person emotionally and cognitively.

When such tools are being used in classrooms, ideally the teacher steps in at the right moment, assesses progress and judiciously moves the child along to a new level of experience. The teacher is replaced during episodes of problem-solving, but intervenes in order to link the series of episodes together into a conceptual map. Children working with such a teaching tool have a great deal of freedom to move at their own pace, follow individual thinking patterns and build a repertoire of experience, largely without a teacher.

On the other hand, it can be argued that the problem-solving child can manage more easily without a teacher than without the support of friends, for he or she will need to get through a stage of uncertainty, of trying out tentative guesses. Herbert Thelen (Thelen, 1981) calls this a plastic, playful period and argues that social support, preferably from a small group of friends, is needed; otherwise the learner may retreat into old, comfortable explanations and learn nothing.

Some learning aids, however, incorporate the principles that Westbury advocates while allowing pupils to work in groups. Comparison of two different kinds of computer-assisted learning is interesting. The first example enables the students to learn in groups. Many of Westbury's principles apply, but not, I would say, principles 1, 3 and 8. A computer program can be used to simulate the interaction between variables and the real world, for instance the ecological balance in a pond. Is there some number of fish that can be caught without upsetting the capacity of the remainder to reproduce and maintain a population? The model is explained to the children, who then try out different numbers of fish caught and the computer calculates the outcome. The children thus approach the notion that the forces of nature can be represented as a set of regular relationships — a very difficult notion to teach. The outcomes *could* be calculated by arithmetic or from tabular charts, but much less efficiently and with much less fun. The limitation of this use of computers is that children gain no idea of how to make the computer do a similar thing in different circumstances: its processes remain mysterious. The computer is used as a learning aid rather than being itself the subject of learning.

The second example, I think, uses all Westbury's eight principles. In using the computer language LOGO, children are involved, albeit in a minor way, in inventing small programs of their own, giving them names, and 'teaching' the computer those names so that they can make the computer repeat the tasks and possibly add them to other tasks they have invented. In this way much of the language by which they operate the computer arises from their own experience. They invent it, share it and control it. Moreover, each move they make can be stored on a personal disc so that they can look back over their own thinking processes and see how they have travelled. The essential qualities of LOGO (and similar languages) are that it can carry out and visibly signal the result of each separate instruction the child chooses to give it (instead of signalling merely the result of several complex calculations), and the words it uses are much like ordinary language. As a result the child has considerable power to control the computer and, moreover, to control the pace, direction and subject matter of the learning process. In the long run, through such processes, people might understand and control technology rather than suffering inertia in the face of technological determinism.

So far I have discussed learning materials in classrooms. Students learning 'at a distance', my second case, have only occasional or no access to a teacher. Does this result in a greater degree of independence? Open University courses provide interesting instances and have been well researched. Students work at home at times they choose, but within the time span of an Open University course, which has a population of students moving together towards an assessed outcome, the pace and the sequence must be controlled and students must be shown the sort of outcome expected of them. As a consequence, phases of independent problem-solving activity tend to be set into a framework of time limits and self-assessment activities. The result of this for some students is that they run out of time and avoid the activities altogether, so they produce the outward form of learning rather than experiencing the process that the course designers hope for. The university's need to pace students, however, is not an attribute of distance learning but of its need to assess. The sequencing of students' activities, on the other hand, would be regarded as necessary and inevitable by nearly all distance teachers.

It cannot be claimed that the sort of social support recommended by Herbert Thelen can be packaged, but there are several approximations such as informal tuition, telephone tuition, encouragement to form self-help groups, dialogues in printed text, simulations and strategies for encouraging students to solve problems rather than merely hoping to be given an answer. Nevertheless, the evidence is that a steady band of students reject interaction and face-to-face tuition and prefer isolation, and they are no less successful in achieving course grades.

Critics both outside the Open University and inside (Woolfe and Murgatroyd, 1979) point out the similarities between its pedagogy and that of the conventional universities. 'Instruction in both kinds of universities can be characterised by reference to what in other contexts has been referred to as "packaged knowledge". By packaged we refer to the idea that knowledge is perceived as being a well defined commodity which is external to the individual student and has its own taken for granted validity . . .' In short, it is tempting to think of autonomy as an outcome of unstructured teaching and high structure as an adjunct of institutionalised packages, and so to argue that institutionalised provision is unavoidably restrictive. Later I shall argue that this is not necessarily so.

By contrast, my third case, students who learn independently of any institution, define their own problems but use highly structured knowledge through structured information storage systems. Stephen Brookfield compared a small group of independent learners with a small group of Open University students by means of in-depth interviews. Seven of his 25 independent learners described amassing a wealth of data which they found they had to classify and catalogue for easy retrieval, ten referred to using libraries and eleven claimed extensive private libraries. They seemed tolerant, temporarily, of partial solutions to their problems, rather than experiencing feelings of defeat and failure. They relied for support on peer and interest groups and chance encounters: 'The kinds of difficulties a researcher might regard as problems they regarded as enjoyable challenges, or interesting diversions . . . ' (Brookfield, 1982). The Open University correspondence course students, on the other hand, rarely strayed outside their courses, which they regarded as self-sufficient. They generally liked the design of course material and 'the sequence of student progress and the element of self-assessment built into the units . . . met with approval'. But they reported learning difficulties, were aware of labouring under constraint, pressures, fatigue and anxiety. The two groups of students were different in almost all respects. Among his conclusions Brookfield remarks, not quite as strongly as Woolfe and Murgatroyd, 'Correspondence courses can encourage convergent and conventional thinking'. This careful statement is undeniable. But are the study characteristics he has described evidence of it? In my view, no. Students' discomforts about their current ways of learning are symptoms that could arise from a variety of causes. In particular, they may be evidence of dissatisfaction with their current learning style and a portent of change to a new and better style.

So, I come to the fourth and last aspect of independence in learning that I wish to explore: the capacity to choose one's own learning strategy. This, of course, involves the students in reflecting on their own learning processes and in knowing and recognising the appropriate use of different strategies. Whether 'appropriate strategy' means that the student should adopt the style the designer intends or not is a point at the crux of several recent studies by the Open University Study Methods Review Group. What students perceive learning to be, the style(s) they adopt, and the outcomes of learning are related to one another, the group reports; at present it is too soon to say quite how. They also find that students fall into two broad groups — those who try to remember and those who try to understand — and there is evidence of transitions between the intermediate stages of these more or less sophisticated conceptions of learning. By contrast, from the teaching point of view one can indicate a rough spectrum, at one end of which are educational designers whose aim it is to produce materials which lead students inevitably to follow a particular learning style (and this leads to meticulously detailed construction of texts) and, at the other end, designers who feel that students should be left to work on relatively raw material in their own way. Also, some academics feel that there is not merely a range of learning styles but a hierarchy (allocating low status to rote learning and sequenced instruction and conceiving of Bloom's taxonomy as a grading system rather than a catalogue of possibilities), whereas others feel that appropriateness for purpose is what matters, and they choose accordingly.

THE PROCESS OF LEARNING

To me, the most interesting aspect of all this is the frequency with which designers of Open University courses invite students to be *aware* of the learning process or processes available to them at a given moment. A precise example is to be found in the course 'Risk', the designers of which have inserted into their texts activities called 'Probers' which invite and enable students to recognise their own level of present understanding of an issue, and specifically their degree of certainty or 'justified uncertainty' (Lefrere, Dowie and Whalley, 1980). The list of examples that follows is not at all systematic, but gives the flavour: an idea is presented and re-presented in different media and the student is invited to re-examine her or his first conception in a new way and told why; a batch of materials is presented in loose-leaf so that students can re-assemble them for different learning purposes; a summer school students' handbook explains the processes and purposes of small-group discussions and the anxiety of uncertainty it may create for some students; a course sets out to distinguish what it calls 'minimum learning objectives' for each section of the course text, arguing that students who can be confident of identifying the essential core will feel *less* need to play safe in the ways they tackle the text as a whole. The essence I wish to identify is the frequent use of strategies that point out to students ways of reorganising the acts of reading, looking and listening for different learning purposes.

Parallel to this anecdotal evidence of the way course designers behave are studies by the Study Methods Review Group on the way students behave — parallel in the sense that neither is directly consequent on the other. Paper No. 5 is especially relevant (Gibbs, Morgan and Taylor, 1980) and I quote its conclusions below.

> Some attempts to train students in study skills seem no more than educationally repressive devices to fit students within such constraints. Consequently, we would argue that practical attempts to help students adopt more purposeful and effective approaches to their learning should have the following goals:
>
> 1. The development of students' conceptions of the learning process. By this we do *not* mean heavy theoretical teaching on learning, but a student centred facilitation of students' own awareness.
> 2. The development of students' awareness of the nature, and *purposes* of study tasks. By this we do *not* mean training in the use of specific techniques.
> 3. The development of autonomous flexibility in adopting learning approaches appropriate to particular study tasks and learning intentions, and the emancipation of students from habitual and limiting approaches.

It seems, on balance, that autonomy in learning is not synonymous with distance from a teacher. Nor does the independent choice of one's own course necessarily lead to a style of learning that generates autonomy. Much of the responsibility lies with the designers of learning materials.

CONCLUSION

Packaged teaching is not necessarily correspondence schooling. Learning in isolation does not necessarily confer independence; on the other hand, it does not necessarily lead to convergence. People can have more choice of what they learn and how they learn. Communication media can extend and intensify experience so that what is learned becomes more socially and personally relevant. These are educational questions, but their political implications are far from simple. There is no educational reason why the whole curriculum should not be available at many levels and in many teaching modes in packaged form. This would require an even distribution of resources across and beyond the present curriculum. (Note that it is financially much easier at present to develop school packs on computer-assisted learning than any other.) It would also fundamentally undermine the archetype by which young people are socialised at present.

The advent of high-technology communication will affect the way we teach, whether for good or for ill. If its impact is not to be inhibiting, pedagogy must take more account of how to design material. The profession then might develop two branches. One branch would need academic skills, graphic skills and editorship, knowledge of media and their analysis and evaluation and pedagogical uses. The other would need academic skills too, and could also rely on new, cheap capacities (such as video disc) for immediately accessible and very attractive information. But primarily they would be able to extend counselling and facilitative roles. For this they would need to know how people learn. Their students would be drawn from diverse age groups and community backgrounds, and many present assumptions about readiness and maturity would be challenged. The controlling function of classrooms could then wither, collegiate structures would emerge and the custodial role of schools would be very difficult to preserve. All these changes would benefit not only the citizens of the future but also an economy in which the need for a manufacturing workforce with robot-like qualities is fast disappearing.

REFERENCES

Brookfield, S. (1982) Independent learners and correspondence students, *Teaching at a Distance*, No. 22.

Clark, C.M. and Yinger, R.J. (1979) *Three Studies of Teacher Planning*. Michigan: Institute for Research on Teaching.

Galton, M., Simon, B. and Croll, P. (1980) *Inside the Primary Classroom*. London: Routledge & Kegan Paul.

Gibbs, G., Morgan, A. and Taylor, L. (1980) *Understanding Why Students Don't Learn*, Study Methods Group Report, No. 5. The Open University.

Jones, B. (1982) *Sleepers, Wake*. Brighton: Wheatsheaf.

Lefrere, P., Dowie, J. and Whalley, P. (1980) Educating for justified uncertainty, *Aspects of Educational Technology*, **14**, pp. 61–65.
Riesmann, D. (1951) *The Lonely Crowd*. London: Yale University Press.
Thelen, H.A. (1981) *The Classroom Society*. London: Croom Helm.
Westbury, I. (1973) Conventional classrooms, 'open' classrooms and the technology of teaching, *Journal of Curriculum Studies*, **5** (2), pp. 99–121.
Woolfe, R. and Murgatroyd, S. (1979) The Open University and the negotiation of knowledge, *Higher Education Review*, Spring.

FURTHER READING

Papert, S. (1980) *Mindstorms*. Brighton: Harvester.

14

The political context of educational alternatives

Marten Shipman

Placing proposals for educational reform within the context of economic constraints, political pressures and parental hopes is a depressing business. Yet as I listened to the participants in the conference on Alternative Educational Futures and read the papers presented in this book, I appreciated afresh the great advantage of our distributed, disseminated, decentralised educational service. The reformers, whether schemers or dreamers, at least have grounds for hope. It may seem optimistic to map out radical alternatives to contemporary schooling in a contracting, and hence entrenched, service, yet somewhere there is the exception that may become the norm, the dream that may become reality, the radical that may become established. We may not be able to predict which innovation will blossom, but at any time it is possible to look back twenty years and identify major changes that have taken place in and around the schools. These changes are not dependent on shifting a massive central educational bureaucracy. Indeed, marked recent changes such as the switch to mixed ability grouping in primary schools or the abandonment of corporal punishment have spread from the margin, from teachers free to experiment and often jealous of their right to do so. Somewhere there will be an experiment that may be picked up and swept into popularity.

At the start, however, it is right to warn that this school-based activity is as political as that engineered by the Secretary of State for Education, or the Chairperson of the Education Committee in an LEA. Teachers are aware of the benefits and the costs of changes such as releasing more information to parents, promoting more self-assessment, or holding all pupils to a common curriculum to statutory leaving age. They are also aware of the feelings of administrators, inspectors, advisers, other teachers, pupils, parents and employers, and the power that these producers of and customers for education can bring to bear to support or oppose change. To ignore this political context when considering alternative futures is to ensure an excessively high mortality among the innovators as they go over the top. The future will come from innovations negotiated and implemented in economic and social contexts. It will be affected by the powerful, often conservative and usually, but naturally, selfish attitudes of parents towards the well-being and future of their own children. This chapter attempts a summary of the alternatives proposed. But it also places them in context in order, it is hoped, to show how the death rate among the innovations can be reduced.

Five questions follow. Why are alternatives required? What binds together the alternatives proposed? What barriers are in the way of their implementation? Who would benefit and who would lose if they were implemented? Which are the most promising ways to attain the supported alternatives? These are tough questions, for the costs of educational reforms, in human as well as material terms, are sometimes high and usually unpredictable. The despair of the reformers is not the result only of the barrier they meet, but also of the tendency for the best of motives to result in the worst of consequences for just those sections of the population who can least afford to have their competitive position in the market-place for labour further reduced.

WHY ARE ALTERNATIVES REQUIRED?

My name has only ever been requested to support one cause: the retention of *Listen with Mother*. But the educational professoriate have joined the great and good to call for reform of secondary education. From the political left come demands for the overthrow of capitalism, but while this is being planned, there are demands for more democratic schools, for unstreaming, for no corporal punishment, for less competition and for more social education. From the political right come demands for a return to Victorian values, but meanwhile, for merit to be rewarded, for greater efficiency in teaching, and for more accountability in the way school resources are used. There is no unity in the changes recommended, except that they are needed. In 1982, in the 'Platform' series in *The Times Educational Supplement* were pleas for the abolition of public examinations, their replacement by profiles, and their extension to all children. The government of schools was to be in the hands of the teachers, the local community, a mix of parents and employers, or LEA-nominated personnel. Schools should be places for vocational preparation, for leisure, for active involvement in democratic decision-making, for the exercise of effective management skills.

The most authoritative statement of the reasons why secondary schools need reforming has come from Husen (1979). He gives four major sources of strain in contemporary schooling. First, it is isolated by bureaucratisation, unionisation and the prolonging of school life. Second, it frustrates the young because not even success guarantees a good job on leaving. Third, there is confusion over the relationships between schooling, the family, the mass media and other educative organisations. Last, schools have become increasingly out of step with the rapid changes taking place in the world of work. Many of these trends have been elaborated by Wragg in Chapter 1. Most of the contributors to this book take one or more of these aspects as a start for their recommendations. In addition, however, there is a stress on the need for more humanity, more support and scope, a priority summed up in Hemming's 'confidence-building curriculum'.

Thus there is a combination of instrumental concern with the short-comings of schools as a preparation for working and social life and an expressive concern with schools as environments for children to mature in with confidence. Significantly, there are few mentions of primary schools. The concern with older children in secondary schools is not just a reflection of current high unemployment or the pressure of public examinations on the curriculum, important as these are. It is anxiety over the measures that teachers find necessary when hundreds of reluctant learners have to be confined in reasonable order in a cramped and inconvenient space. The articles may seem critical of teachers, but they are concerned with the uncivilised conditions in which many have to work, as well as with the boredom of many pupils. This emphasis on the absence of joy, the stunting of expression and the regimentation and competition within schools has a long pedigree in the romantic movement. Kitto, introducing a conference of Education Otherwise in April 1982, called it the product of the hippie generation as parents. In this sense the absence of reference to power, to costs and to the division of labour was expected. It is salutory to be reminded that schools are about more than material rewards.

WHAT IS BEING RECOMMENDED?

The proposals in this book fall into two broad categories. First there are those pressing for the de-institutionalisation of education. This is an obvious case, for there is an absurdity in education, which is concerned with individual learning and expression, being organised in large institutions through procedures that have limited variety. There is a range of contemporary views, from stout defenders of large schools to fervent deschoolers. In between are many, such as Harber, Hargreaves and Watts in this book, who would leave the institution of schooling but democratise, liberalise, open it to the world outside.

The reforms recommended in the book are also liberal in another sense. Unlike those on the left who write off schools as instruments of state propaganda serving to make the injustices of capitalism seem natural, or those on the right who would use schools to promote national and racial exclusiveness, the contributors here have faith in the capacity of the service to be reformed instead of destroyed or placed under a dictatorship. That optimism is also reflected in the reforms suggested, which are in the learner-centred direction. There is a faith in the capacity of the individual if only it is allowed to blossom. Confidence-building, the expressive arts, empathic social relations, love and care are supported as means of releasing human goodness and energy. There is nothing here of original sin and little of schools as agents of social control. It is a rosy view of the world, far removed both from the roots of elementary schooling in the need to ensure salvation by punishment if necessary, and from the problems of teachers as dirty-workers, struggling to keep order because that is the condition in which a little learning can take place.

The remaining recommendations are also optimistic. The plea is for the open school: parents will be welcome inside, and children will be encouraged to work outside. Education will take over from schooling. Of course, parents are usually more conservative than teachers, and would be likely to treat radicalism in organisation and curriculum as they treated the teachers in the William Tyndale Junior School, by withdrawing their children. It is not unfair to say that if the proposals in this book were implemented, the schools concerned would face rapidly falling rolls as parents sought to secure an academic schooling elsewhere. But the selfish urges of parents, like sin, are illiberal and consequently ignored. In the end the world is changed by dreamers. It is difficult to select the likely successes among saints, but some of them have changed history, even if they have rarely lived to see it happen.

WHAT IS IN THE WAY OF ALTERNATIVE FUTURES?

There are many sources of institutional inertia in the education service, and these are discussed below. But it also has to be remembered that schools, as they are currently organised, suit those who benefit. There is over forty years of evidence, from Gray and Moshinsky (1938) to Halsey, Heath and Ridge (1980), to show the unequal way in which rich and poor are rewarded through schooling. But the latter also show how the service class, including the teachers, have passed on their advantages through the use of both maintained and independent schooling. The organisation of schooling is defended by those who benefit from it. These are usually the politically articulate. Those seeking alternatives because they suspect that schools are unsatisfactory for the majority have to face the human urge that underlies the defence of an unfair service. The drive to benefit one's own children overcomes most principles or leads to double standards. Only the very rich can afford to be relaxed over the schooling that can benefit their children, and the academic power-houses of contemporary public schools indicate that the anxiety to achieve accreditation is widespread. There is no reason why the poor should not hope that schools will give their children a taste of the gravy.

The most powerful constraint on innovation where it is usually most desired arises from the intimate link between schooling and the market for labour. Repeatedly the grip of public examinations on the secondary-school curriculum is the focus of reform, yet the reason why examinations have been given such a position is rarely considered. Only Lynn Davies' account of education in the Third World shows the crucial factor which lies behind schooling that is made meaningless for the many so that a few may be rewarded. Education is meshed into an advanced division of labour in a country like ours, and the schools serve to differentiate between children. That is the role of examinations. It is also a feature frequently criticised by authors in this book. The competition within an academic curriculum is seen as restrictive and often demeaning, as few succeed and many fail. As teachers sort children out from an early age, they are also playing their part in the differentiation. The process starts early: before children select their examination streams they have a clear idea of their place in the pecking order, and the evidence has been given to them in school (Hurman, 1978; Ryrie, 1979).

The failure to take this link between the division of labour and schooling as central results in wishful thinking and the setting of wrong targets. If public examinations could be abolished this would not free children or the schools from the process of differentiation: the rationale of schooling is sorting out. It is inconceivable that children could remain undifferentiated, for that not only would leave the job to employers or to higher education, but would probably favour the children of the rich even more than schooling does at present. Furthermore, O'Keefe (1981) argues that the poor realise the competitive situation as well as the rich and have as much right to be able to compete. Neither Marxists on the left nor Conservative hawks on the right make the mistake of ignoring the connection between school and work, but reformers tend to utopianism, ignoring not only this powerful constraint on schooling but the realisation among poor and rich alike that it exists. The grip is felt by teachers, by politicians and by parents as they fret about their children. This anxiety is not confined to secondary schools: the parents who withdrew their children from the William Tyndale Junior School were not prepared to risk involvement in a curriculum that might have weakened chances in the competition for qualification. Black parents who pay for Saturday schools are making up for what they feel is a deficiency in maintained schooling (Stone, 1981). They are interested in basic subjects, in marketable skills. They are doing just what the rich do when they buy an independent schooling for their children: they are trying to secure a decent future in a highly competitive world of work.

The remaining factors that stand in the way of reform are more fully appreciated and have contributed to reversing many of the budding movements towards alternative education. Falling school rolls have weakened the bargaining position of the education service against the competition for resources by other public services, particularly those serving expanding needs such as the growing number of the very old or the unemployed. Similarly, the series of economic crises throughout the 1970s led to policies from Labour as well as Conservative governments of cuts in public services to protect investment in the private sector. This economic policy has necessitated decisions that have adversely affected the public services, and education in particular. The education service was not in a position to resist pressure at national, local and parental levels; Labour and Conservative governments responded to what was seen as a widespread concern with the basic subjects and with accountability that further exposed schools to influences that were often re-actions against attempts to move from traditional curricula.

These factors adversely affecting education have been well documented (see, for example, Lawton, 1980), but the underlying impact on the education service, particularly on the possibility of local innovation, has been neglected. First, education is particularly vulnerable during contraction because over two-thirds of expenditure goes on wages and salaries. Teachers, once appointed, serve for up to forty years. Rightly they resist redundancy and being switched between schools, but each teacher appointed, each school built, each innovation funded, is an investment for years ahead. When sustained contraction follows expansion growth is built into the service, and that can be funded only by cutting elsewhere. Those cuts fall on the small proportion of funds used for books, materials and the resources for innovation, which are cut disproportionately.

The second underlying factor comes from the different impact of cuts at national, local and school levels. Pupil-teacher ratios had fallen nationally every year to the end of 1982, yet many LEAs were having to allow class sizes to increase by not appointing new teachers. At school level, the loss of a teacher could mean drastic retrenchment. Thus decisions are easy to make in the DES, difficult to implement in the LEAs, and can be a disaster in a school. Schools now tend to be staffed by LEA definitions of the basic curriculum. Instead of school-based initiatives, the LEA defines and protects the core. But LEAs are also inhibited in acting independently because resources, provided mainly through the block grant from central government, are insufficient to fund even existing commitments. Decision-making is forced from the schools to town or county halls, and from there to the DES. From there the basic decisions are referred to the Treasury.

WHAT WOULD BE THE COSTS OF ALTERNATIVES?

One of the unfortunate consequences of much educational innovation is that it harms just those children who need help most. This is not merely the result of the middle-class source of much reform. Marxists can see this reform as ideologically tainted, or at best peripheral to the interests of the working class, because education is seen as part of the apparatus through which the state establishes conditions where injustice and inequality come to be seen as natural rather than the result of repression of one class by another. But you do not have to believe in the determination of social relations by economic structure or the inevitability of its overthrow by force to appreciate that reforms such as the ending of selection for secondary schooling, the extension of statutory schooling, the liberalisation of the curriculum and greater investment in the service have not benefited the poor. Yet every reform is premised on claims to greater justice or equality. Reformers have to hesitate and ask the awkward questions, why is it that the consequences of reform are often unanticipated and why do they frequently turn out to further deprive the deprived? We may not have admired Rhodes Boyson, either as a head teacher or as a politician, but his opposition to most reform has been based on his justifiable suspicion that alternatives to the traditional school organisation and curriculum are often designed, whether naively or blindly, ignoring the political pressures around schools and the anxieties of parents about the future of their children. The costs of alternatives have often outweighed the benefits. The reactionaries have been right too often for alternative futures not to be weighed most carefully.

When the possible costs are weighed against the possible benefits, the difficulty in moving to alternatives that will not penalise vulnerable groups becomes clear. Hemmings, Hargreaves, Harber and Watts in this book are all concerned with the way schools are organised around subjects that become little empires. But if those subjects are abandoned in inner-city comprehensive schools and preserved in the suburbs and independent schools, the gap between rich and poor will widen. The independent schools have read the market for high-prestige jobs with remarkable success, as have the service class as they seek a maintained education that will be advantageous to their children (Halsey, Heath and Ridge, 1980).

All the proposals in this book would have opportunity costs. Educating children out of school and forms of flexischooling could add to the adverse effects of the Assisted Places Scheme by removing the children of motivated, articulate, knowledgeable parents from the maintained schools. These alternatives are often inconceivable for the poor, for they require resources, knowledge, a place to do school work at home, and parents who have the skill to help and who are not exhausted by manual labour after a day's work. Inevitably the alternatives, whether in or out of school, would leave the poor in the same unfortunate position as now while the rich still creamed off the university places and the top jobs, through monopolising the A and B grade examination results, while a few took a chance outside the conventional schools. Fewer than 5 per cent of children go to independent schools, but they take 28 per cent of university places.

There is a danger in this neglect of costs in innovations that accounts for the glacial progress away from rigid subject boundaries and examination-bound schooling. Teachers are cautious and *The Times Educational Supplement*'s surveys of opinions (*The Times Educational Supplement*, 1977, 1983) suggest professional conservatism about such aspects as the abolition of selective schools and of corporal punishment. That conservatism is based on the same suspicion of the costs of change as Harold Wilson's 'over my dead body' comment on the phasing-out of grammar schools. It is popular to deride 11-plus selection tests and public examinations, but they have a degree of objectivity that is a safeguard for the poor, the unconventional and the non-conformist. Anyone who has had a switch from examinations to continuous assessment knows the peril to the student who doesn't toe the line and deliver the expected goods on time. If selection is inevitable at some stage in a child's career because there is an advanced division of labour in the market for jobs, care has to be taken not to replace universal by particular criteria. The alternative to public examination can be patronage. The alternative to testing can be nepotism. A meritocracy may be inhumane, but it is probably preferable to and certainly more just than the early Victorian values that selection and promotion by merit replaced.

WHICH ARE THE MOST PROMISING WAYS FORWARD?

Awareness of the constraints on education innovation and of the political factors which bear upon the service is not a reason for despair, but a way to exert influence effectively. The reformer, particularly of secondary education, has one powerful support at present: there is widespread concern to promote a better way of organising the schooling of the young, and the forces of reform are liable to coalesce. The message is clear: stay around and keep pitching, for sooner rather than later something is going to give; but meanwhile scheme as well as dream.

There is another important clue to the most promising ways forward. Unless you are a historical materialist or belong to some other group with a pessimistic, deterministic creed, you can take comfort that for all the talk about the state, systems, factors and forces, changes come about through the actions of individuals or groups of humans working together. This involves obtaining and using political leverage, but this is a nation of pressure groups. When doubts arise remember the mothers of young children who organised the pre-school playgroups. Remember Henry Morris and the community schools movement, and the pioneers who were inspired by Montessori or Froebel. There are examples in this book from Boulter, Diamond and Stevens. There is always change and it comes from two or three gathering together and setting about influencing others.

In the chapters of this book there is a spectrum of alternatives. At the low-risk, incremental end is Geffen's account of the use of educational technology as a support for independent learning: the potential of the

Open University outside conventional degree courses has hardly been tapped as yet. Meighan presents a range of contacts between parents and schools that could make up flexischooling. He also supports Geffen in seeing the rapid developments in information technology as a way of networking learners into support services. Education Otherwise acts as a focus of mutual aid for parents who are interested in learning at home.

The frustration of parents and teachers who want alternative forms of schooling arises partly from the apparent obduracy of local education authorities as they interpret the law, particularly with regard to attendance at school. This is understandable, particularly at a time when resources are scarce and schools have falling rolls. But there are also advantages in this situation for the reformer. First, LEAs are not monolithic, either in their defence of the existing organisation of schools or in their rejection of attempts to adopt unusual arrangements for the education of children. They are at present subject to rapid changes of political leadership as younger members take over. As rolls fall, schools have to be reorganised; small rural schools are an obvious example. Under these conditions LEAs may consider supporting parents who can make a good case for educating their own children or co-operating to arrange to educate a group. At the meeting of Education Otherwise at the University of Birmingham in April 1982 there were representatives from LEAs discussing the possibility of linking parents educating their own children with local schools so that support and advice were available. All LEAs are under financial strain and are being forced to look for alternatives that are more cost-effective, particularly for pre-school and post-sixteen education. Furthermore, the teachers have not dug their heels in. Since the Plowden Report in 1967, most primary schools have strengthened links with parents (Cyster and Clift, 1980), and central government has supported this through the Education Act 1980.

The problem often lies in the mutual suspicion between parent and administrator, or parent and head teacher. The solution has to be through collaboration. LEAs are busy bureaucracies, with procedures that enable them to organise schools effectively. Exceptions are at best a nuisance, at worst a deflection of effort from mainstream activities for the majority. Similarly, head teachers will often detect special pleading in a parent's approach. Of course there are stubborn bureaucrats, teachers and parents, but most will try to be helpful if the procedures that avoid special pleading are followed. It is impossible to know your luck; some time you may get the timing just right.

It is to pressure-group politics that those looking for alternatives usually have to turn. It is easy to gather a few people together and think up an appropriate acronym; CASE, ACE, PRISE, ESTEAM, STOPP,

CREEM and SOS are a few better-known examples. Many never have a title, but the group involved use their contacts effectively. There is always someone who knows someone who is on the council, who knows the spouse of the MP, who entertains the chief education officer, or who plays golf with the head teacher. The impression of a middle-class coterie was intentional, as pressure-group politics tends to leave out the poor and ignore class conflict. But trade unions, trades councils and the Labour Party are also important potential allies. Somewhere there is access to those with influence, and a hand on the levers of power is not very difficult to find.

Finally, the distributed influence in the English education service is an advantage to reformers, a source for hope; teachers can move forward without waiting for instructions from above. A contemporary growth area, for example, is involving parents in listening to children read from books sent home with children. LEAs pioneered progressive primary, comprehensive and community schooling. Watts and other innovatory head teachers could experiment because LEAs such as Leicestershire were supportive. The DES, under successive Secretaries of State, both Labour and Conservative, has moved to encourage greater involvement of parents in the government of schools and to promote the release of more information from schools and LEAs. Accountability may carry a threat to professional autonomy but it is also a promise of more of a say for parents, employers and others. Above all, when the balance of interest is being disturbed, the chances for new alignments and hence alternatives increase.

This has been a sceptic's view of the chances, the costs and the benefits of seeking alternatives in contemporary schooling. That search is widespread. Husen's analysis of shortcomings in *The School in Question* was written by a Swede about schooling in the West (Husen, 1979). Davies in this book has shown that similar problems exist in the Third World. All are concerned with the anachronism of cooping up active adolescents in buildings that have changed little from those designed for young children beaten into submission in more brutal times. We have raised the age of leaving without changing the context or content of schooling or its public examination. When the crisis over unemployed school-leavers arrived, the initiatives were left to the Department of Employment and the Manpower Services Commission. There is widespread recognition of the fact that schooling is an unsatisfactory and uncivilised experience for many children and staff. The ways forward have to be political because schools are locked into the arrangements for the distribution of jobs and hence the good and bad things of life. Choices have to be made and costs balanced against benefits, but human endeavour does change human organisation. We can identify the successful movements of the past, and our children will be able to trace those organised by our generation. In that liberal sense, powerfully stated in J.S. Mills' *On Liberty,* the scepticism is misplaced. Somewhere alternative futures are being shaped.

REFERENCES

Cyster, R. and Clift, P. (1980) Parental involvement in primary schools: the NFER survey, in Craft, M., Raynor, J. and Cohen, L. *Linking Home and School.* London: Harper and Row.

Gray, J.L. and Moshinsky, P. (1938) Ability and opportunity in English education, in Hogben, L. (ed.) *Political Arithmetic.* London: George Allen & Unwin.

Halsey, A.H., Heath, A. and Ridge, J. (1980) *Origins and Destinations.* Oxford: Clarendon Press.

Hurman, A. (1978) *A Charter for Choice.* Windsor: National Foundation for Educational Research.

Husen, T. (1979) *The School in Question.* Oxford: Oxford University Press.

Lawton, D. (1980) *The Politics of the School Curriculum.* London: Routledge & Kegan Paul.

O'Keefe, D.J. (1981) Market capitalism and nationalised schooling, *Educational Analysis,* **3** (1)

Ryrie, A.C. (1979) *Routes and Results.* Sevenoaks: Hodder and Stoughton.

Stone, M. (1981) *The Education of the Black Child in Britain: The Myth of Multi-cultural Education.* London: Fontana.

Times Educational Supplement (1977) Survey of teachers' opinions, 2 September.

Times Educational Supplement (1983) Election '83, 27 May.

Index

Ability, 66
Accountability, 5, 176
Agency, 86–7
Assessment, 5, 8, 10, 16, 18, 24–5, 44, 133
Assisted places scheme, 173
Attitudes, 4–5
Authoritarian people, 143–4
Authority, 55–6
Autonomy, 22, 150, 151, 154–65

Baker, J., 109
Barnet College, 145, 151
Behaviour as experimentation, 84–5
Behaviourist theory, 82
Bias, 47–8
Black Papers, 78
Boiteko (self-help), 69
Boyson, R., 173
Bullock Report, 30
Bullying, 144
Bureaucratisation, 168
Butler, R., 146

Cape Verde Islands, 71
Capitalism, 167, 168
Carey, J., 87–8
Carpenter, E., 146
Child-centred education, *see* Education
Child development research, 85–6
Children, individuality of, 123, 129, 131
Christianity, 126
Citizenship in teaching, 40–53, 127
Community, 133, 138–9
Community problems, 66
Competition, 127, 167, 168, 170
Computers, 6, 8, 127, 147–8, 155, 159–61

Conceptual maps, 159
Confidence, 13
Conservatism, 173
Contracts, 145, 150
Co-operative enterprise, 69, 70, 73, 76
Corporal punishment, 149, 166, 173
Correspondence courses, 145, 146, 161
Countesthorpe School, 97
Courage, 13
Creativity, 106
Campaign for State-Supported
    Alternative Schools (CSSAS), 50,
    91–104, 150
Culture, 126–7, 141
Curiosity, 13
Curriculum, 8–10, 14, 27–38, 95, 154
    broad, 120, 123–7, 164
    confidence-building, 13–26
    hidden, 143, 146
    negotiated, 33–4, 57–8
    subjects of, 17, 32, 60, 173
Curriculum 11–16, 30

Dartington Hall School, 108
Davy, Sir H., 15
Departments, 35, 58–9
Deprivation, 134
Department of Education and Science
    (DES), 100
    and WES courses, 120
Deschooling, 105–16, 144, 146, 151
Discipline, 120, 127, 137
Discrimination, 101
Distance teaching, 157, 160, 163
Diversity, 152
Down's syndrome, 118
Dyslexia, 118

Education—
  in Africa, 64
  authoritarian, 44–5, 144
  in Botswana, 68
  for capability, 106, 115
  child-centred, 118, 168
  community, 8, 10, 50–1, 60–1
  compensatory, 132
  creative, 21–2, 106
  in Cuba, 64
  decentralised, 8, 166
  democratic, 40–53, 91–104, 144, 152, 167
  economics of, 171
  '14–18', 33
  further, 34
  goals in, 101, 103, 104, 115
  health, 22
  higher, 10
  for leisure, 67
  for life, 141
  location of, 146, 150
  orientation, 20–1
  origins of system, 131
  in Papua New Guinea, 64, 66
  personal and social, 17, 32–3
  political, 40–53
  political context of, 166–77
  with production, 63
  romantic view of, 168
  for self-reliance, 63–7
  in the Seychelles, 65, 66
  for subsistence, 60
  in Tanzania, 65

Falling rolls, 7–8
Families, 131–142, 146
Faraday, M., 15
Fathers, 134, 137
Finance (of education), 172, 173
First-hand experiences, 124
Flexischooling, 129, 143–53, 175
Foundation for Education with Production (FEP), 67–9
Four Avenues School, 99
Freud, A., 79
Friere, P., 70–1
Froebel, F., 174

Grammar schools, 173
Group work, 11

Health education, 22
HMI, 29–31, 102
Holt, J., 106, 113
Home-based education, 105–16, 114, 118–29, 143, 147, 150

overseas, 121–3, 125, 143, 146, 149
Horizontal rotation, 36
Housing, 136
Huxley, A., 15

Ideologies of education, 151
Inner London Education Authority (ILEA), 102
Illich, I., 105, 108, 109, 114
Incentives, 75
Independent study, see Autonomy
Industrial democracy, 43–4
Inequality, 170
Information systems, 143, 147, 155
Institutionalisation, 169

Janov, A., 109
Job-sharing, 98

Kant, I., 83
Kelly, G. A., 83–6
Knowledge, 2, 4–5, 16, 56-7, 147, 156, 161

Lambert, R., 110, 118
Language skills, 124, 125, 131, 137
Learning—
  as fun, 127
  as process, 81, 91
  strategies, 157, 161–2
  without a teacher, 146
Leisure, 2–4, 146
Lister, I., 111–12
Literacy, functional, 63, 70–2

Manifesto for change, 146
Marxism, 40–1, 172
Mass media, 147, 155
Mead, G. H., 85
Microprocessors, 127, 143, 147–8, 155
Montessori, M., 79, 174
Moral development, 87–8
Morialta High School, 99
Morris, H., 174
Mothers, 134, 137
Manpower Services Commission (MSC), 6, 176
Mulberry Bush School, 79

Narration, 124, 126
Neill, A. S., 79, 105
Nottingham University, 2
Numeracy, 71–2, 74–5
Nyerere, J., 65, 75

Observation, 125–6
Open mind, 46–7

Open University, 143, 145, 146, 149, 151, 160–2, 175
Orthodoxy, 144

Parental Involvement Project, 74, 131–42
Parents, 54, 74, 92–3, 97, 100, 101, 109–10, 112, 118–29, 131–42, 143, 146, 149, 150, 167, 169, 175
Parents National Educational Union, 118–29
Pastoral care, 35–6
Physical maturity, 3
Picture study, 121, 126
Plowden Report, 131, 158, 175
Political cognitive development, 50
Political groups, 3, 175
Political ignorance, 41–2
Political issues, 66
Political power, 168
Political skills, 42–4
Politics (educational), 166–77, 175–6
Pringle, K. M., 140
Psychological theory, 79, 81, 82, 83
Psychology—
    Freudian, 19
    gestalt, 18
    personal construct, 83–6
Punishment, 99

Qualifications, 4
Questions (use of), 5

Regimentation, 144, 150, 168
Rensburg, P. von, 68
ROSLA, 105
Rural economies, 64
Russell, B., 79, 144

Sandwell Project, 134–42
Schooling—
    comprehensive, 27–38
    legal issues in, 100
    selective, 171, 173
School leaving age, 3, 55
Schools—
    alternative, 97–103
    community, 100
    Danish little, 100, 115, 144
    financing of, 102, 103, 115–16
    independent, 49, 173
    multicultural, 150
    Saturday, 171
    uncivilised conditions in, 168
    within schools, 144, 150, 152
Secondary Schools Community Extension Project (SSCEP), 66
Self-direction, see Autonomy
Self-esteem, 92
Self-help, 64–7, 69, 107, 134, 138, 151
Self-interest, 74

Sidney Stringer School, 50
Sixth forms, 7
Skills, 4–5, 19–20, 42–4, 66
Skinner, B. F., 83
Social class, 4, 172–3
Social control, 169
Socialism, 65
Society—
    changing, 146
    democratic, 152
    diversified, 152
    pluralistic, 152
Streaming, 100
Syllabus (structured), 123–4

Tanzania, 65, 69
Teacher(s), 54–62
    age, 8
    attitudes, 135
    Evaluation Project, 2
    role, 65, 76, 151
    semi-specialisation of, 11, 58–60
    shortage of, 64
    training, 36–7, 62
Teaching, 128, 155, 157–9
    authoritarian, 65
    democratic, 45–8, 65
    by parents, 128, 137, 143, 149
    resources, 59, 149
    style, 68
    team, 59
Technology, 6, 64, 127, 147, 154–65
Textbooks, 147
Third World, 63–77, 170, 176
Thomas Bennett School, 49
Trait theory, 81–2, 88

Unemployment, 2–4, 6, 148
Unionisation, 168
Units within schools, 150
Urban situation, 134
USA, 4

Victorian values, 174
Visiting homes, 133–5, 138

White Lion Street School, 97, 102
Work—
    collapse of, 146–8, 156, 164, 168
    ethic, 156
    experience, 73
    at home, 148
    and school, 171
Worker co-operatives, 70
World-wide Education Service (WES), 118–29, 146

Yorkshire project, 107–9

Zimbabwe, 69